Praise

'"Bossing it without burn ___ ___ion call every entrepreneur needs to heed. Mike Buonaiuto lays out both the urgency of the need to answer our call to build, and the importance of doing so without sacrificing your life. *Founder Therapy* is the right medicine at the right time for every entrepreneur.'
　— **Jerry Colonna**, CEO of Reboot.io and the author of *Reboot: Leadership and the art of growing up*

'No human wishing to start their own organisation should do so before reading this book. This is an essential read for all compassionate entrepreneurs – and an even more essential read for those who need to develop their compassion and empathy.'
　— **Chris Folwell**, Head of Diversity, Equity and Inclusion for Europe, The Middle East and Africa, Uber

'No matter what stage you are at in your entrepreneurship journey, *Founder Therapy* is the book for you. These fifty lessons are packed with honest conversations that you should be having with yourself right now to build emotional resilience.'
　— **Karishma Gupta**, Founder and CEO of Eslando Circular Fashion

'A must-read for aspiring or current founders. Mike has trodden the path from startup to scale-up and has found a unique way of sharing his experience and learnings, tying personal stories to practical guidance. As Mike states: "Don't build a beautiful cage". *Founder Therapy* will certainly help in ensuring you remain healthy in mind and create a business with social and authentic purpose.'
— **Richard Thornton**, angel investor and Operating Partner for J12, a VC seed-stage fund

'This book clears the path for every founder looking to step into their power – because who you are is how you lead. And investing in how you lead is just as important as what you're leading.'
— **Julio G Alvarez**, Executive Coach and Founder of Out in Tech

'This is the book every modern-day founder needs. Distilling compassion and expertise into fifty lessons is a godsend to anyone who's serious about growing their business.'
— **Stephanie Melodia**, Founder of Bloom

'*Founder Therapy* is a truly authentic and transparent homage to founders from any background. It's a deep unravelling of the different journeys we go through, not simply as founders, but as individuals – because the distinction is so very important.'
— **Thomas Panton**, Founder and CEO of Canopey

'*Founder Therapy* is a rare, humanised handbook to the founder journey that emphasises, contrary to current popular opinion, you are as important as the company you're building.'
— **Sam Moss**, Co-Founder of Stocked

'This is the definitive playbook of emotional and business stability for budding founders.'
— **Adam R Brown**, psychology and neuroscience at work expert. Founder of Sparqpath

'One word: relatable. A must-read for anyone looking to start a business or for someone looking to take their business to that next stage.'
— **CJ Glover**, Managing Director of In2Group

'The journey to building a successful business can be fraught with many challenges and hurdles. This guide will serve you well no matter the stage of your journey, helping you to stay true to your mission and purpose and to succeed within the entrepreneurial game, without compromising your wellbeing.'
— **Carol Lathbridge**, Co-Founder of Tiwani Heritage

FOUNDER THERAPY*

No-bulls**t ways to boss it
without burnout

Hey Evie,

keep Climbing

keep building!

Mike

MIKE BUONAIUTO

R^ethink

For Lauren and Ed,
who taught me to compassionately nudge
my comfort zone.

I'll be forever grateful.

Contents

Foreword

I first met Mike Buonaiuto on the final leg of his founder journey with Shape History, coaching him on his exit strategy. It was the final act in his extraordinary journey as the leader of an organisation that laid the blueprint for how to tell the story of social impact.

He looks set to shape history once again, this time for the next generation of founders, with this timely book on how to build your dreams without wounding your wellbeing. It's arrived just in time to help the next generation of UK founders avert a path to burnout.

Studies have now irrefutably linked higher rates of mental health issues to success-driven entrepreneurship. Why does this matter? Private sector businesses in the UK turned over 4.14 trillion British pounds in 2020, a rise of a trillion pounds in only eight years.[1] It seems that 64% of people are looking to start a business. The rate of entrepreneurship in the UK is set to grow and it remains the lifeblood of our competitive position in the global marketplace.

Entrepreneurs are a unique tribe of hopeful, idealistic and creative life forces with an ability not only to see what other people have not yet imagined, but to also bring that vision into being. Our world, like never before, needs to nurture this tribe – to understand what they need to succeed and step up to meet their unique requirements.

This book and the lessons shared within will be the life raft you will reach for when facing one or all of the fifty challenges contained within its pages. It is the book I wish I'd had on my nightstand over the many years of my own founder journey.

The birthing and raising of an enterprise is a profoundly creative experience. It is at once a deeply personal road and also a daringly exposing act of vulnerability. We stand in the arena of life risking it all, in a high-stakes game of succeed or fail. We are the frontier folk, the pioneers of our generation, the possibility seekers and the disrupters, making the necessary changes to improve the experience of human life on this amazing planet. We are the visionaries who can stare into a blank space and populate it with the stuff of dreams. This rare talent and beautiful expression of the very best of what it means to be human must be supported practically and emotionally at all costs.

Our responsibility, as members of this exclusive tribe, is to get acquainted with what it is in our unique makeup that enables our high tolerance for risk. To get busy building our awareness of what we need as individuals, to keep powering that 'high performance'. To set our own boundaries and stick to them. To slow down sufficiently to notice the pseudo-urgency draining our energy tank, pushing us out of balance and way off course.

In this important book, Mike's searing honesty about his own mental health roadblocks reminds us that our failure to recognise the flickering embers of our own potential burnout can cost us more than our business. It can cost us our health, our relationships and, sometimes, our lives.

I was a female co-founder of a company that grew rapidly within its first five years, acquired by a FTSE 100 company in its sixth year of operation, rolling on to become an equity partner in what is now a billion-dollar global business, the earnout from which became my burnout until I pulled the cord on my parachute. Looking back, my burnout began as I sat surrounded by lawyers, signing the papers for the sale of my business, while seven months pregnant with my second child. The urgent, relentless pursuit of control, and the belief that how it all turned out was all 'on me', took its toll on my body. After a painfully short maternity leave and the death of my father, I was back at the wheel, grinding out that earnout, playing superhero at home and in the office. One running injury after another triggered crippling back pain that stopped me in my tracks and potentially saved my life. My body said no, and my mind eventually caught up. Today, I work with founders, leaders and those hoping to push the boundaries of their potential to do so without mortgaging their health and happiness.

This book matters. The output of entrepreneurialism benefits everyone. Founders are armed with an enviable vision and a high threshold for risk, yet we need the practical and emotional support to realise our true potential. This book will hold your hand through all the milestones of the real-life MBA that is your founder journey, but will also provide you with the emotional wellness tools to founder-coach yourself on that journey, too.

Eva Reynolds
Founder of nORTH Business Consulting and Exited Founder of Open Health Group

Prologue

The book you wish your boss had read

You made it. Welcome. This book is for you – for founders, for leaders, for directors and for anyone building a business that doesn't want to burn out in the process. Wherever you are on your journey – be that early-stage development, prepping for investment, initial scale, rapid growth or even considering or orchestrating an exit – thank you for picking up this book and considering your wellbeing and development. I promise it will be a vital step to becoming a more conscious leader, helping you make more purposeful decisions that provide sustainable growth for your clients and customers, for your people, for the planet, and, most crucially, sustainable *for you*.

Your company is something you will need to invest in, day in and day out, for however long is required to reach your goals. It's a marathon. To do so, you'll need to put into practice strategies and ideas that are going to make sure you can stand the test of time. The lessons within this book will help you get there. There's no reason that a marathon cannot be conquered as several sprints. Let's make things more manageable.

Throughout the process of scaling and selling my own company, alongside working now as a business performance coach and senior advisor, I've discovered trends that link us all; lessons that connect almost every founder and every startup, which, if followed and considered, can and will vastly affect whether your company, and in turn you, reach your potential.

The trends and challenges ahead of us are universal. From green energy to affiliate marketing, from food and drink to clothing design, from branding to building development – the lessons in this book have come up time and time again. We're not nearly as alone as we often feel or think we are; we're not lonely in facing our challenges, nor are we lonely in our ideas to achieve better.

This book will cover all the basics, from operations, resourcing, sales and marketing, to investment, cash flow, fundraising and selling. It will also cover crucial lessons often ignored while we strive for success, such as founder-wellbeing, team morale, and conscious leadership development. These lessons are the secret to whether your business survives or fails.

The process of building your company can and should feel a little like therapy. It should challenge you, and teach you things about yourself you didn't know existed. Too often I see founders autopiloting through their work, and their lives, living up to unsustainable expectations or role models, fuelled by past experiences that may only lead to unfulfillment and unhappiness. I hope that the lessons in this book help us all to switch off that autopilot mode, and instead consciously build our companies the way that *we* want.

There's no getting away from it: your startup is and will continue to be an extension of you; an augmentation of your own identity. If proper attention isn't taken, alongside becoming the reflection of everything that makes you powerful, your business may, unfortunately, begin to mirror things that are problematic within you. It's our job as founders and as leaders to be ready for that balance, understanding what is powering us and then using that knowledge, in turn, to make good choices.

It's become increasingly clear that our 'high-performance' generation has a real problem with burnout. In a recent study at UCSF, Dr Michael Freeman interviewed and worked with over 1,000 entrepreneurs, founders and business leaders from across diverse industries, backgrounds and cultures. His findings alarmingly linked higher rates of mental health issues to success-driven entrepreneurship.[2]

Within his study, almost *half* of entrepreneurs and founders reported living with a mental health condition such as depression or chronic anxiety. More strikingly, three-quarters of the half that didn't suffer directly, said they came from families significantly affected by mental health concerns. Most interestingly, when compared with the general population, entrepreneurs were found to be twice as likely to have depression, three times as likely to abuse substances to self-medicate, six times as likely to express symptoms of ADHD, and eleven times more likely to sit on the bipolar spectrum. Perhaps most tragically, the results suggested that mental health issues do not just affect the individuals themselves, but, like a disease, low self-esteem, anxiety and depression are infectious, with most co-workers, close friends and family members also experiencing symptoms.

It would be interesting to understand whether these outcomes are due to correlation or causation. Are entrepreneurs more likely to display these traits because they are entrepreneurial or because they founded enterprises? Regardless, there does seem to be something fundamental about the neurobiology of those that push themselves to their absolute limit to achieve entrepreneurship, for they are far more likely to exhibit underlying mental health concerns, which, in turn, can spill out into potentially destructive behaviour.

Through more qualitative research, Freeman's team discovered that founders are also far more likely to display impulsive, compulsive or addictive behaviour. Ambitious individuals are, in a sense, he argues, dopamine junkies. This can range from behaviour society would traditionally see as self-destructive, such as gambling and consuming fast food, drink and drugs, but also traditionally celebrated behaviour, such as serial entrepreneurship, cumulative risk-taking and persistent workaholism. Freeman suggests starting a business itself is not only an example of an extremely high threshold for risk but that there is also a need for it. In short, success and the extreme lengths founders will go to in order to achieve it is a socially acceptable dopamine hit.

Sound familiar? Perhaps slightly? I'll be honest, this *was* me. For too long, artificial urgency was powering my business. I thought I was at the wheel but I wasn't consciously in the driving seat. My hypervigilance for money and speed, from a childhood of bullying and financial problems, meant my company had not only to be the *most* profitable, but also had to reach profitability faster than any business I knew. It made the early years super successful, but at what cost? It wasn't sustainable. While the business became internationally renowned, winning awards, securing mammoth contracts with global organisations and scaling multi-million-pound revenues, I started rolling into work more times hungover and exhausted than not. I would snap at employees, micromanage to a fault, and dread the monthly payroll. I was burning out and the signs were all there. It could have been as subtle as the shot of coffee I felt I needed before every pitch meeting, or as glaringly alarming as the time I stood staring at the tracks as my train rolled into Waterloo Station late at night, inches from my unsteady feet.

After years of work, much of it spent working alongside many experts, I've been able to recover from what was fuelling my early years in business. I now help others to do the same, using the very lessons contained in this book. These lessons not only helped me recover, but they also empowered me to grow a successful international company, and then exit it. When put into practice, they will help you both automate your startup and build sustainable models that will allow your company to scale independently of yourself. As you embark upon this journey that so often feels unfamiliar, threatening and even lonely, while at the same time so full of wonder, potential and inspiration, your organisation has to fulfil its potential without you or those around you burning out.

So are the stakes just much higher than they used to be, or is something else going on? This book will first cover the current societal backdrop, the pool from which your company will draw its clients, customers and people. We'll then explore some vital lessons for preserving the wellbeing of founders and teams. Following that, we'll dedicate some hefty page real estate to leadership and culture, and then discuss the tactics to help you pitch your business in the early stages to customers and investors. We'll next dive into operations, cash flow and budgeting, and lastly we'll cover crucial advice that will hopefully help pull you across the finish line and sell your business through a successful exit. This could be via an MBO (Management Buy Out), an EOT (Employee Ownership Trust), or a Trade Sale. Along the way, there will be a healthy amount of anecdotes and stories, from my own experience and from several others'.

Most of all, I hope this book will help you become the type of leader you want to be, and that your business will reach its potential. Think of this as your pocket-size co-founder. Feel free to scribble all over these pages. The lessons in this book will only work if they resonate with, and are relevant to, you.

This is the first step to understanding what makes you tick as a founder and leader. Welcome to that journey.

Introduction

You want to start a business now?

You want to scale a business in today's climate? When it's never been harder to secure investment and when investors are understandably spooked by unsteady and uncertain markets? When financial, physical, and even emotional security has been proven to be at an all-time low, inspiring a lack of confidence in consumer spending? When buying homes, having children and other milestones which signalled success and stability to the previous generation now seem so much more unattainable than they once were? When recruitment strategies that proved successful in the past now struggle to retain and remunerate people on their true worth? When climate change requires businesses to rapidly adapt not just to account for shareholder value, but also the value of their social impact and climate footprint? When you look around and discover that you're part of a generation that has lived and continues to live through the shadows of a seemingly endless cycle of crises? From the 2008 financial crash and the austerity that followed, to the division of a referendum and the financial fallout from Brexit. Then there's Covid, the climate, rising inflation, the record cost of living, and finally the increasing chances of cross-globe conflict brought about by increasing resource scarcity and available living space.

You want to start a business in the face of all this? Good. I'm here to tell you – that's good. **Like a plant growing stronger and more resilient in the places it's most under pressure, in the startup world testing times stress-test timely ideas.**

Businesses do not sit outside of society, in a safety bubble all by themselves. Companies and organisations, just like people, sit firmly within a culture and society; they serve it and are served by it. They can be afflicted by its problems and privileges, or they can inflict and influence them.

The businesses that understand the demands of today's global society and, more importantly, how it affects their local communities, will be the businesses and the leaders who survive and thrive to scale undisputed heights of startup success over the next twenty years.

Those of us that can ride out the storm and create businesses that respond to our generation's most crucial problems will also be the companies that attract the most investment. The startups that understand how mainstream media news cycles operate, and how the national conversation is constructed, will be the businesses that can interject that conversation with their own voice, scale accordingly and pay dividends in the future. And I'm not just talking about financial dividends. All of this context will help prepare you to run an organisation that responds to today's world without wounding your wellbeing, so let's look in particular at the ecosystem in which you're starting a business.

A recent study by Deloitte, an international professional services network, found that, unlike the generation before, and for the first time in living memory, buying homes, having children and other 'success markers' of adulthood do not top young people's ambitions.[3] Moreover, earning a high salary and being wealthy ranked second on a list of goals, but came last in the list of achievable outcomes. While in 1990 the average house price was just over £57,000 and the average household income was £20,000, in 2020 the average house price has risen to £237,000 but the average household income sat at £37,000.[4]

When we look at the school system, we largely see an institution that prepares the vast majority of us to be employees rather than employers. During those crucial years of our development, rather than being inspired with free thought and creativity, on the whole we are taught the opposite of what it takes to be sustainably successful. **We're taught to not make a mistake, to do as we're told, to follow the rules, to take tests by ourselves, and that there's only one right answer.**[5] We leave school scared of making mistakes, determined to succeed alone, and frustrated when the rules don't work out for us, all while being paralysed by competition and finding the right answers. Our society's approach to education has created entire generations of people who are unprepared for the adult world, not adapted for sustainable success, and not ready to lead others.

The truth is that the majority of us at work are now completely overwhelmed by stress. A study by the American Psychological Association found that almost one-third of all adults are so stressed that they struggle to function in day-to-day life.[6] More specifically, over half of young people – those entering the workplace as new graduates in particular – feel anxious about inflation, the government and the rapid cycle of seemingly never-ending crises.

This is the workforce you will be empowering as a founder and a leader. This is the support network you will need to build for and with. This is the society you have come from and now must serve.

How do we do this? First, let's acknowledge that the environment we live and work in plays a huge part in determining our mental health. Johann Hari, in his book *Lost Connections*, examines the core factors behind our generation's affliction with anxiety and depression.[7] Hari highlights the findings of British researchers George and Tirrel that, more than anything, the contributing factors to poor mental health lie within environments that breed isolation, loss of social interaction, uncertainty of the future, and lack of familiarity.

The very places we spend the most time – at home and at work – deeply impact our wellbeing. **It's our responsibility as founders and company owners to understand this; to be able to build helpful and supportive workplaces that aren't just mindful of society's problems, but actively look to combat them.** We must do this for others, but also for ourselves. This is the verbal contract we sign with the world when we choose to start a business within it.

When we look at the types of companies that are currently gathering the most interest from investors, we see that they are by far those most suited to weathering and responding to societal concerns. This includes companies that are:

1. Contributing to solving the climate crisis.

2. Providing radical transparency for people to make informed choices, ie, their spending habits.

3. Dissolving boundaries to authentically bring people together around shared life experiences.

4. Challenging the centralisation of power by providing decentralisation of data.

5. Rethinking the way businesses communicate their social impact to the world.

There's one more trend that I'm seeing repeated in conversations: increasingly, companies attracting the most attention from investors are those which veer away from the model of growth for growth's sake and instead value efficiency of profit and purpose. Until very recently, we lived in a world where company valuation and return on investment were calculated primarily on a multiple of revenue that far exceeded any expectation of profitability, but with increased volatility, **profitability at any scale, not just at scale, is now becoming an ever-more important factor for investors.** (This is explored in much more detail in the 'Operations and Budgets' chapter.)

I'm aware we've started with doom and gloom. It's intentional. I do this so you're under no illusion, but also to contextualise the lessons contained in this book and make sure you're best prepared to consciously build a business that responds to the growing needs of society. Deeply understanding the world within which our business sits is the first step to safeguarding our wellbeing as we work.

The truth is, while we've never quite experienced a time like this, it's not all bad. It's never been easier, for example, to find like-minded folk to begin your startup journey. It's never been quicker to set up the platforms required to amplify your company's voice. It's never been safer to access the support you need to accelerate your business forwards. Much of this will be covered in the book, including the financial incentives that are easy pickings for founders and investors to get going in a cost-effective and conscious way.

Let's crack through these fifty lessons. Ready?

PART ONE

FOUNDER AND TEAM WELLBEING

1
Know Your Profitable Poisons

It's said that three out of every five startups fail. I'm here to tell you that isn't (just) down to poor cash flow management, or (just) down to under-investing in their product. Failure is almost always because the founder didn't invest enough in understanding their own wellbeing and the wellbeing of their team – their drivers, their triggers – discovering what is truly powering them.

Many founders think that if they just push themselves and those around them just a little bit harder, and if they can just ignore those feelings of guilt, shame and pressure for just one more year, success will surely follow. Startups are run by human beings, though, and human beings are run by their emotions and feelings.

Just like therapy, if you don't get ahead of it, it will get ahead of you.

'How have you been complicit in creating the conditions you say you do not want? And how have those conditions in turn served you?'

This is the vital question asked by Jerry Colonna, an early godfather of Silicon Valley now turned seasoned business coach, to some of the world's most successful CEOs and startup entrepreneurs. Jerry has been an investor, an executive and a board member for 100 companies for almost twenty years, and now helps entrepreneurs lead with humanity, resilience and equanimity. He is the CEO of Reboot. io and the author of *Reboot: Leadership and the art of growing up*.[8]

His question is often where I start in coaching sessions, helping founders, CEOs and leaders unpack their own sense of wellbeing in a bid to help them discover what is truly powering them forwards. It's a tricky one, because it hints at something unspoken; something hidden. It hints at something we're never taught or encouraged to think about, let alone say.

Are there parts of us we do not like which actually make us better or more effective at our jobs? Are there actions we take that make us unhappy, that we take anyway because they help build our business? And if so, why?

For me, the answers to those questions lie in our understanding of safety and security – namely the type of safety and security we build companies for; the things about the world we want protection from. For most people there are three big ones: financial, physical and emotional security. Sometimes one overpowers the others, but increasingly, given today's societal and cultural issues, it's a mix of all three.

'The more something threatens your identity, the more you will avoid it,' writes Mark Manson in his book *The Subtle Art of Not Giving a F**K*.[9] He's right. We will avoid answering these questions. We will avoid delving into our mental health, and not just because of the veiled impression of 'killing it' that we're taught to present to the world – to fake it till you make it. It's because so much of our identity in those early stages of building a company is wrapped up in the identity of the company itself, that questioning one is impossible without questioning the other.

Here's the thing: these questions are important because, without a doubt, there will be things powering your company and team which stem from behaviours or habits you do not like; from childhood and early adulthood lessons you learnt, even subconsciously, about building financial, physical and emotional security. We want to avoid you autopiloting your way through building a business, unaware of what is powering you forwards, especially if it stems from a place which is less than healthy, because those unhealthy behaviours can begin to be mirrored back at you in your team's culture.

'We hide our wishes for safety and security and turn them into a wish for success,' said Jerry Colonna when we met during preparation for writing this book. It was a video call over lockdown as he's now based in Boulder, Colorado. 'All entrepreneurs try to make their wishes acceptable,' he continued.

These wishes often come up in coaching sessions. I call them our **profitable poisons**. They are the things we picked up along the way; behaviours we learnt to keep us safe, which in turn benefit our businesses and make us successful.

For instance, I grew up in a household where money was often scarce, and where my father spent every penny he earned scaling his small, local company on building a life for his kids. He wanted my siblings and me to have access to the type of education and security he didn't have as the child of first-generation Italian immigrants. The result of this was that I developed a belief that money equals success, but hardly ever equals happiness, because growing up there was never much of it and what little there was, was often packaged up with a lot of stress and pressure. As an adult, I carried with me from childhood a hypervigilance around money, which in turn would make me shit-hot at picking out the details of P&L (Profit and Loss) reports. In fact, while building my business,

I had been known to spend evenings and early mornings tearing through financial reports, line by line, focusing on microscopic details. This resulted in my business having a highly astute robust cash flow, which of course made us super successful in the early years. Every penny had to go on making the business as efficient as possible, because I didn't know where the next penny would come from.

The problem with this is that it resulted in my business's finances being fuelled by anxiety, which would end up seriously affecting the relationships I had with accountants, and in time, senior staff members. The very thing that was making my business successful was being powered by something problematic. It was my profitable poison. It would also begin to destroy my wellbeing, and force me to try to live with a constant nervous anxiety that I tried to normalise for the sake of success. I thought it was an acceptable trade – it wasn't.

I got the help I needed. It turns out, the trick was not to abandon the behaviours altogether, but rather build a self-awareness which enabled me to consciously use my skills of hypervigilance without letting them damage my wellbeing or the wellbeing of my team. In short, just understanding where these feelings were coming from and what was fuelling my behaviour was enough for me to learn how to change things. These are now the lessons I share with other founders, CEOs and leaders.

The opportunity to create a positive response from trauma is known in the psychology world as Post-Traumatic Growth (PTG). While Post-Traumatic Stress is suppressive, PTG is transformational; it's thriving from the trauma, which acts as a catalyst for action with purpose.

We cannot live a life governed by what protected us in the past. So many founders build through or in response to trauma. They experience huge injustice and want to fix things for others, so they build startups that make that happen. This makes them successful because others can feel the authenticity and integrity in their mission. What I've learnt most about my experience working with founders, and also being one myself, is that trauma cannot power you to scale; it cannot take you the whole way. It must transform and find reconciliation. It must lead you to make conscious choices.

Like many of my generation who choose success and over-achievement as a way of masking our deep uncertainty about the world and insecurities about ourselves, it's important to acknowledge that, at some point, we've all grieved for a life we were promised as a child and then not received as an adult. It's ok to admit that. The deeply demanding world we were born into, and the immense insecurities that have therefore plagued my generation specifically, have damaged so many who are still with us, and all too many who are sadly not. While grieving is natural and vital in processing change, we often forget that healthy grieving should always end with reconstruction, acceptance and hope. It's time to do that work, for those we love, for those we work with, but largely, for ourselves. It's time to reconstruct, accept and build towards success in a healthy way – in a way that doesn't lead to burn out.

2
Toxic Shame Vs Timely Shame

We've all felt that pang of shame or guilt. Often it's in the pit of your stomach or for me, strangely, it's felt in my chest. It can spur on anxiety or uncertainty about the world or the choices we're making within it. It can lead to flashbacks, to getting lost in a single moment, overthinking or overplaying the eventualities of a choice.

Feelings of shame are often built in our early years. Research from Harvard University shows that our brains develop rapidly during the first years of life, quickly developing our mapping system like a sponge absorbing knowledge in order to both survive and thrive.[10] We're learning faster than we ever will throughout the rest of our lives, often when we don't know we're learning at all. Shame is a part of these lessons and is largely taught inherently by our parents' actions to keep us safe.

If you grew up in a house with an open fireplace, for example, and you got too close to it, whether it was lit or not, your parents likely encouraged you away from it, perhaps even scolding you for getting too close. As very young children we want to keep our caregivers happy. We want their validation, praise and attention, for they are the source of our security and safety. Over time, you learn that approaching the fireplace didn't make your caregivers happy, it didn't bring you praise and, most importantly, it made you feel shameful. You'd then begin to avoid it. This is 'timely shame' and it's helpful.

Toxic shame is developed in response to being taught that something fundamental about ourselves is wrong or dangerous, usually from a parent, and then reinforced by wider society. It starts in the same way, by not receiving praise or validation for certain actions or behaviours and then increasing to receiving outward negative responses from others. It could be for growing up gay in a largely heteronormative world, for example, or growing up female in a world which often favours men. The list, sadly, is far too long. **Toxic shame develops when we learn that something fundamental about ourselves is incorrect or wrong – something we cannot change.**

Now as an adult, especially an adult building a business, it's vital to begin to distinguish feelings of shame within yourself – mainly which feelings are helpful and which are not. Toxic shame vs timely shame. All feelings of shame can either be used to hold you back or push you forward, but what type of shame you are responding to can determine if you're pushing forward in a healthy or destructive way. One is going to be far more repeatable than the other, day in day out, for much longer. Fuel yourself with toxic shame and you'll burn out far more quickly.

Ask yourself, how are you making your day-to-day decisions about the security and safety of yourself, your team and your business? Are these decisions in response to feelings of inadequacy, guilt or worry – and why do you think that is? In contrast, what areas of your life and work are you fuelling with timely shame? That feeling of slight pressure, perhaps, to build a career that's stable and secure for yourself and your loved ones? The feeling of needing to prepare for the future, to build the kind of life you want, perhaps for your children?

The trick is not avoiding shame altogether. **Shame can be helpful. Shame can be a useful nudge in the right direction.** The trick is to understand which feelings are toxic and which feelings are timely, and then build behaviours and habits around healthy shame while disregarding the more unhealthy feelings you hold. They may have carried you this far, but do you really need them to power you forwards, now you're conscious of them? The answer is most definitely no.

3
Pick Your 'Hard'

While growing up, my dad would often say, 'when you buy something, remember you're buying a problem'. Ever the cynic, it was his little way of teaching me that while the joy of acquiring something you need or want can be great, in the end it will end up costing you more in time and effort than it ever did originally in money. Things go wrong. Nothing ever lasts. Cars need servicing. Technology needs new parts. Houses need upkeep and bills need paying. The more you acquire, the more you will spend, in both your time and your money – maintaining, nurturing and preserving. It was probably one of the most useful lessons he ever taught me, because to this day, when I hover over the 'buy it now' button online, or get my card out of my wallet, I think to myself, what will this choice end up costing me in time, in the long run, and will that be worth it?

The exact same questions need to be asked, and answered, when building a business. What problems are you buying? Every choice you make as a leader to acquire more may in turn cost you and your team more – in time, energy and effort. Every decision you make to scale your company further will eventually mean you need to make further choices; choices which will weigh on your most precious resource of all – your time. This isn't a reason to get lost in indecision, fearful of taking a step forward or making a new commitment for fear of the pressure it might bring you. Far from it. It's a reason to make conscious and informed choices.

Rather than autopiloting forwards, scaling your business just for the sake of scale, instead, try to remain conscious of which 'problems' you are acquiring in your pursuit of success. Try as hard as you can to proceed with perspective. This will stop you and your team becoming, at worst, overburdened or burnt out, or at best, surprised or unprepared. In coaching sessions, we call this 'picking your hard'. Nearly everything about scaling a business, especially at the start, can be extremely challenging. It's about having the self-awareness to know it will be hard, and that's ok, that's normal. This sets a realistic expectation you can build upon and is critical to becoming a compassionate and decisive leader.

4
Defend Your Peace

There are no easy roads to success, whatever success looks like for you, but to avoid burnout or our actions weighing heavily on our mental health, we have to know why we're in the game to begin with. What are we trying to achieve for ourselves and for others? A lot of the time when I ask this question to founders, I get the same responses: to create a positive change in the world, to create a form of financial freedom for themselves and their families, to do something better than they have seen done before. These are all valid, but knowing your purpose often runs deeper than that. I'd actually go as far as to say these are, in effect, distractions from the true reason why each of us actively chooses the harder path in the bid for 'success'.

To find the *real* reason you're willing to wake up every day and do something as hard and challenging as starting and running a business, next time you are feeling overwhelmed at work, rather than asking yourself what extent you are willing to go to in order to reach success, **ask yourself to what extent are you willing to go to in order to reach peace?** This should shift your perspective.

Success can bring us many things and it can be used to justify putting our bodies through extreme circumstances. If only we can work that little bit harder, push ourselves that little bit further, we'll reach that level of 'success' we're looking for. Let's be brutally honest, if success is not bringing us peace, in a world where peace is becoming an ever-more scarce commodity, what on Earth are we striving for?

Your time at peace could be anything at all that makes you feel relaxed, happy and truly your authentic self, and what's more, it doesn't have to be time spent away from work. Part of your job could actually be when you're at peace, and if you're an entrepreneur this is likely the case. It's whatever activity (or non-activity) that's personal to you, that calms the cortisol in your brain (our body's stress hormone) and gets you feeling truly and utterly peaceful.

If you're unsure what your 'peace mode' is, ask yourself two questions:

1. What do you find yourself doing when you lose track of time?

2. What have you done since a child that's always made you feel truly fulfilled?

That will be it.

For many people, the patterns of behaviour they find most comforting are identical to those they most enjoyed when they were kids. In this way, I believe, our 'peace modes' may even come somewhat pre-installed, or certainly heavily influenced by childhood pastimes, when our world was a simpler place.

Tragically, in our current world of workaholism, we likely spend far less time in our 'peace mode' than our body and mind truly requires and deserves. We're sucked from it, pulled into more pressing things; things which feel urgent or necessary. Success and peace in today's world are often like either side of a coin – gambled, flipped, but impossible to manifest at the same time.

Defending your peace is critical to growing your business without burnout. What's more, true success is being able to choose when you switch on and off your peace. This took me years to learn, and even longer to remember to put into practice. I had to make it a habit. So often our vision of success is the excitement, the speed and the energy of power, influence and autonomy. But all of that is nothing if you cannot use it to decide when you are, and when you aren't, peaceful.

How do you defend it? Your 'peace' needs to be booked in and scheduled. Just as we block out the time for meetings, events, deadlines and pitches, so should we be scheduling out time for our peace. Once it's in the diary, you should be defending it – with everything that you've got. When we take time to accommodate the moments when we are most peaceful, we can truly understand the value of the time we spend when we are most at stress.

A word on this is, however, important. As we grow, the value of our peace can change. It could be due to family, children, travel – anything. Your capacity for stress and capacity for peace shift over time, so while you should defend it at any cost, try to be open to also reassessing its boundaries as often as feels natural.

Try defending your peace for a week and I guarantee that you will understand what I mean when I use the word *defend*. Those around you, and perhaps even yourself, will almost certainly begin to undervalue the time in your diary for peace – and you'll quickly start to see it being attacked and encroached upon. Traditionally, this time isn't seen as useful to building a business – but I'm here to remind you it should be. **The whole point of building it is to provide opportunities for you and for others to live in your most peaceful state.** Like a fortress, time for peace should never be compromised. Ever.

5
Fight Artificial Urgency

You feel that urgency right? It could be that late-night email that just needs sending, or that deal that just needs nudging over the line. It could be done next week, but next week will have its own set of problems, so it's better if it's done this week – actually, let's get it done tonight, today, in the next hour. Let's just get it done.

Part of your power as a leader, as a founder, is your ability to instil and inspire a sense of urgency in those around you, otherwise, arguably, nothing gets done. Your role as a founder is to set the pace of your organisation, the expectation of acceleration, results and impact. That speed has to be fair, sustainable for the long term and vary at times, but most importantly it has to be *real*. It can be many things – responsive, easily adaptable to shifts and changes, yet also precautionary and set pace with a sense of perspective, but if the speed of your organisation isn't based in reality, you've got yourself a problem.

Too often when working alongside founders and CEOs, this sense of urgency emerges in conversations. Things need to get done yesterday. A tip, I've found, is to interrogate not just the speed of an organisation, but whether that speed or expectation of speed is in fact *artificial*. Let me be brutally honest, nothing chips away at a founder's wellbeing and a team's self-esteem like artificial urgency. This is the feeling that nothing can ever be built or completed fast enough; a hunger that's insatiable for more, at any cost, but with no fixed purpose, mission or measure to reality. Artificial urgency presents itself usually as acute anxious excitement, an exhilarated delirium that pushes you from your comfort zone and heaves you forwards. In small doses it can be helpful, but over time it can eat away at your nervous system.

There is a huge difference between powering success through confident self-discipline vs powering success through artificial urgency. How can we ever keep up with a sense of urgency that always feels unattainable even if our speed increases? Surprise – you can't. You burn out.

I had my fair share of artificial urgency. There was a time at work when I couldn't go into a pitch without popping a codeine and taking a shot of coffee. I needed my brain to be lightning fast. I would stay up into the early hours to work through my to-do list, with hundreds of tabs open at once. I needed success and needed it quickly, and I convinced myself that artificial urgency and chronic stress were the necessary vehicles to help me perform at 'my best'. The reality is that I was constantly forcing my brain into fight or flight mode and expecting the same from those around me. This is an impossible, unrealistic and unsustainable expectation I see replicated, not just in early startups, but in established multinational companies. Everything and everyone is being powered by nervous systems pushed to the brink of performance, reacting to threats rather than opportunities. It gets stuff done – but at what cost?

Success isn't a race and it sure as hell isn't a race you can ever win. The minute one goal is reached another materialises ahead of it. There will always be another win, a bigger team, a larger office, a bigger paycheque. So why do so many of us run our businesses this way? Why are we programmed to constantly work in fight or flight mode, damaging team wellbeing and our own mental health?

To answer that question, it's crucial to look at the science. 'Fight or flight' is an evolutionary response that causes the hormone cortisol to be released when we feel under threat or pressure, which in turn forces a limbic reaction. Our nervous system is essentially an electrical network in our bodies, flicking on and off as our hormones instruct. 'Fight or flight' was useful when we were hunter-gatherers in times gone by, but while modern society has evolved to protect us from such dangers, our brains have not been updated. Our minds therefore have a tendency to flood our bodies with cortisol when other, seemingly benign, hazards, risks or uncertainties emerge; anything from forgetting to pay bills to messing up at work. Over time, with repeated action, it can become our body's learnt response to *any* cautionary stimulus, no matter how threatening, leading to chronic stress. Imagine trying to concentrate when an electrical storm is constantly surging throughout your body; your brain has no means of understanding which neurons are firing correctly and which are firing because everything is.

Powering our businesses (and our lives) with cortisol, while prevalent in much of our world today, is crazy unhealthy. There are two main reasons why. First, cortisol doesn't work alone in our body. Our brain also gives us a healthy hit of dopamine alongside it – you know, the drug that makes us feel amazing? That natural high? That means we likely feel good from working off cortisol and there lies the second problem: dopamine is highly addictive. This harks back to Dr Michael Freeman's research mentioned earlier.[11] Not only is repeated fight or flight at work draining our wellbeing, it's also, tragically, at the same time, addictive. Our brains get a positive response and so want to do it more. **Our minds can become hooked on**

artificial urgency until they can't take it anymore; a horrid habit that gives us results, keeps us repeating the behaviour and yet burns us out at the same time. Ever been looking forward to a day off for ages, only for it to finally arrive and you wake up that morning desperately wanting to open your laptop and reply to that email or tick something off your to-do list? I've often been guilty of this.

So how do we break the cycle? How do we make sure our business isn't powered in this way? How do you create a healthier relationship with work that brings you success but isn't somehow built on an unhealthy relationship with dopamine? Arguably, the answers to these questions lie in every lesson in this book. They are all designed to tackle this pivotal issue that affects, and fuels, so many ambitious folk.

The most efficient way to tackle artificial urgency is to create a new habit, one which reminds you to ask yourself a daily question: what, for you, is enough? I know, we can never have enough. We always want that little bit more. We always want to get it a little bit faster than last time, but really, if we sit back, away from all the distractions, that fever-dream of instant gratification and ever-more available images of unat-tainable comparisons, this question isn't all that difficult. What, for you, is enough?

To help you answer it truthfully, perhaps start by asking yourself, why did you start a business in the first place? What did you want to change about the world? At the same time, what did you want to gain, personally or professionally, from that choice? It doesn't matter what your answer is, just recognise the fact that this answer is indeed personal to everyone. No answer to this question will be identical. Everyone's reason for starting a business is fundamentally different. That's the key to answering what, for you, is enough.

If everyone's reason is personal, so should be the outcome. Along the way, we might get distracted by what we can attain or gain, but if we reconnect with the *real* reason we set about striving for success, we can begin to unpick what, for us, is truly enough. You may have investors who pull you in a direction which is different; who want you to scale faster, to achieve more revenue and profitability. You may have a team that is hungry to take on new challenges, to scale the business in different ways than you do. You may have friendships or a relationship which is causing you to feel pressure you aren't comfortable with.

Getting outside your comfort zone is vital to running a business, as is listening to those around you and giving your team the space to try new things. You'll know when you're working outside your comfort zone because it's the time when you feel most alive, most outside the habitual cycles we live among, most separate from that veil of security in the mundane and predictable.

I've often felt the furthest outside my comfort zone when working and travelling abroad. New environments break you free of old patterns of behaviour and in turn free up your thinking. Change your environment and change your mind. Be aware, though, that constantly striving outside of your comfort zone, while invigorating and exciting, may burn you out. Remember that your business is *yours* and therefore should never stray too far away from providing you with what you feel is *enough*. Enough for now, and enough for the long-term vision. Learning what is enough, for you personally, is the whole point of this journey.

This argument for not constantly striving outside our comfort zone, and not constantly riding the tides of artificial urgency, goes against almost everything we're told today about scaling a company. You can swipe through as many motivational/business/success TikTokers and Instagrammers as you like and you'd probably never hear this kind of advice. For many people, I'd go as far as saying this argument likely feels anti-growth, anti-entrepreneurial, and anti-startup. But the truth is, all of these things should be in balance. They should be different gears you can switch into and out of. To do this, I encourage you to remember that choosing to start and grow a business is a personal choice, and everyone's version of personal success is different. Compare yourself to someone else, someone on a completely different path, and you risk making choices designed for their road rather than your own. **The path most trodden may not be the path that's right for you.**

I see a lot of this sense of urgency, fuelled by comparison, when founders are seeking investment. Often, they will pick a number which feels right to them, based on the conversations they have had with other founders, about the usual amounts investors want to give. They undervalue that each investor should be geared towards their own vision, different to other people's, and, in turn, even undervalue (or overvalue) their own business.

Step back. Take a breath. Remind yourself that everyone's reasons for starting a business are personal to their own journey and therefore everyone's expectations of enough are also personal. Let this define your decisions about speed. Let this define the direction of your business. When you lead with a sense of perspective, you realise that the things you want to achieve will come to you, in time. Success doesn't have to equal instant success. There will be great things you achieve; they might occur now, they might occur later. There are certain achievements which are more suited to a more seasoned age, when your gratitude for greater experience can result in wonders you never thought possible in your youth. There's no race. This is how you build resilience.

6
Crowded Loneliness

'Being a founder is inherently lonely.' This has almost become a throw-away comment in the entrepreneurial world – a half-accepted belief that, in exchange for becoming a leader, you *must* feel loneliness. Sure, when you're at the top of an organisation you can be in the most crowded space, surrounded by others, and still feel incredibly lonely. No one truly knows what it's like to have the weight of an organisation on their shoulders, and moreover, in many work cultures around the world, building a distanced relationship with your boss has almost become the celebrated norm. No matter how compassionate we become in our approach to serving our team's needs, many teams will not want, nor expect, to be friends with their boss, but feeling lonely as a founder isn't inevitable. To sustain ourselves in leadership positions for enough time to grow our businesses, we don't just have to get used to the idea of feeling lonely, we have to find ways to overcome it – and still build worthwhile relationships.

A key step, I believe, is unpicking why, as founders, we can feel lonely. Much of this, in my experience, is battling our needs and wants to be liked by others – something you'll definitely come up against when attempting to lead and manage others at work. The irony is that many of us who start a business do so because of our need to be liked. We create a business to solve our loneliness, not knowing it will only make us feel more lonely.

Stop fuelling your business and your attitude to work with validation. At its very core, entrepreneurship is early-stage innovation; you are therefore a research and development project, not an entertainment attraction. If we get real for a second, we need to realise that innovation is rarely liked, especially at first, and certainly by established contemporaries. Hotels don't like Airbnb. Banks don't like cryptocurrency. Taxis don't like Uber. Cinemas don't like Netflix. The very nature of what you are doing and what you are building is designed not to attract validation, it's designed to attract criticism. To avoid feelings of loneliness, we must first stop looking for companionship through work in the form of validation. You won't get it and you most definitely shouldn't be looking for it, especially in those you hire and work with.

As you build your team, you should perhaps be looking for people you respect and admire, people you can build trust and affinity with, and people who won't make you feel like the smartest person in the room. You should not be looking for people who may make you feel validated – in fact, from time to time they should make you feel a little stupid.

Hire people who can balance both the strengths and weaknesses of your business, and, at a senior level, yourself. Your co-founders and senior team need to understand you exceptionally well, and you need to understand them. You can then rely on each other to both complement but also constructively criticise each other's approach. **You will not feel lonely as a founder if, instead of seeking senior team approval, you instead begin seeking senior team collective feedback.** By this, I mean working with a group of people who can comfortably critique each other without it feeling personal.

In my experience, I've often found senior teams built of odd numbers to be super effective at comfortably critiquing each other. Usually, in early-stage startups, this is three people, approaching the vision of the business from three very different perspectives. One could be creative, for example, the other strategic, the other compassionate. The three people have the same vision and goal in mind, they just have very different approaches to getting there. The cure for loneliness, and in effect, what the likely success of your business depends on, is your senior team's ability to come together, think through eventualities from various opposing angles, and then compromise on a route which feels like the best way forward.

This approach doesn't stop at your team; it's also crucial to become a bit of a collector of like-minded grey-hair outside of your company. By this, I mean finding people who have been there, done it, got the t-shirt, scaled and sold a company, and dealt with their own collection of profitable poisons. A great way to do this is to seek out a mentor or build an informal advisory board. Find people who can advise you and critique you with the perspective of lived experience – who know how it feels to be where you're currently at.

You may feel lonely but your problems are not. Most businesses of a similar size are going through almost exactly the same things you are. We often consider ourselves to be isolated in our issues, as if no one will understand nor want to understand what we are going through – but you may be surprised to realise just how much that's not true. One way I discovered this was during Covid.

At the start of the pandemic, business owners, to put it mildly, had some pretty difficult choices to make; choices many business owners felt like they hadn't signed up for. Who thought about a global pandemic when putting together their startup's business plan risk assessment? Not me!

One of the ways I was able to be decisive during the pandemic was by having regular, informed conversations with my competitors. I would meet the owner of a similar company to mine, who I've known for many years, every month or so throughout 2020, to talk honestly about what we were doing at work, and also privately, to make sure we all survived. During these calls, we would talk openly about keeping our office open for those of our team who were unable to work from home, utilising the UK furlough schemes to avoid redundancies and building projection models which bore in mind the impact of future lockdowns. It was so useful to have someone to talk to who understood almost exactly what I was going through. So often we're taught to keep our issues to ourselves and to certainly not share them with our competitors – but if nothing else, the pandemic taught me **we are so much more alike in our problems than we are different**. This helped me make decisions with more confidence, while also helping me feel a hell of a lot less lonely in making them.

7

Identity Crisis: Who Are You?

As founders and leaders, we feel a sense of identity in what we are building, often tying our own value to that of our company's. This can mean that any criticism or conflicting opinion of the company can be seen as a criticism of, or conflicting opinion about, us.

This is a catch 22, because tying the business's identity to our own, especially in the early years, can help it to become successful. It helps the company resonate with others, standing on your shoulders, piggybacking on your existing brand, network and identity. People need a hand to shake and a face to smile at. Founders who shy away from this risk their business not having an identity for others to resonate with. But – and this is a big but – **just because we tie our**

own identity to our business, doesn't mean we need to tie everything to it. Retaining who you are away from your organisation is vital to not burning out while building it.

As human beings, founders, just like everyone else, are complex individuals. It's impossible to build a business that encompasses 100% of who we are. Where I see this go wrong is when founders tie their work identity to their private identity to the extent that they become one-dimensional beings; where a fraction of what makes them wonderful becomes 100% of who they are, 100% of the time. It's unsustainable. Founders who do this rarely stop to consider what they have given up in exchange for success until it's too late.

As human beings, we cannot operate sustainably for the long term when we are only a fraction of ourselves. Your business is important; it should be one of the principal factors in your life – but that doesn't mean you need to lose touch with all the things that make you awesome just because these traits don't fuel your success. That penchant you have for cooking three times a week might not help you scale your startup on the surface, but try working every week without spending time doing what you enjoy and you'll soon find it hard to scale anything.

Traditionally, we are taught to harness our strengths and turn them into something which can earn us money; take our superpowers and transform them into a business that can empower others to do the same. This is true, but like many things, it's not the whole picture. While we do this to grow our business, there will be 101 other aspects of our identity which bring us and those we love joy. Just because these aspects of ourselves can't or aren't currently being monetised – just because they aren't bringing home the bacon – doesn't mean they should be disregarded or deprioritised. Find ways and build time to invest in *every* part of you that makes you happy.

8
Combat Your Credibility Crisis

Many founders I've worked with have spoken about imposter syndrome – the feeling that we don't know what we are doing or that we are somewhat under-qualified to be in the positions we find ourselves in. So much about the experience of being a founder is choosing a direction without certain knowledge of an outcome, and this can lead us to doubting ourselves. The bigger the organisation becomes, the more it becomes the largest organisation we've ever run, with little experience of anything bigger. If we see the role of founder purely as a builder, then yes, imposter syndrome can be the real deal. Instead, if we shift our focus and cast our role within the organisation not just as a builder, but also as a protector, this can shift our perspective.

Your role as leader is to defend and protect the soul of your organisation, the essence of what it stands for. No one should understand what that 'soul' of your organisation is more than you, and therefore no one is more qualified to protect it. You set the rhythm that others compose to. Especially if you're building something new, something no one else has done in your industry or sector, you will quickly find that **few people are going to give you the certificate of achievement you may think you need to proceed**. You have to give this to yourself. You must stop waiting for validation or permission from others to proceed. *Proceed*.

Decisions will be made together with those you trust and respect, with people who think differently to you, with different life experiences and skills. This is how you limit the chances of those decisions failing, and raise the chances of them resonating with those you serve. But you will fail. This is certain. Your job as founder is not to protect the organisation from failure, or build the organisation itself with nothing but your own hands. Your job is to protect the entity of the business and its reason for existence, and to make sure this is part of every decision made by every part of the business. In this way, it's impossible to feel imposter syndrome because you're simply living out and protecting your authentic vision.

9
Grinding With Gratitude

When we think about ambition and success, and the people who seek it to excess, we rarely think about people who are gracious. Bring to mind any character in any movie who's ambitious and uber successful, and most likely they are ruthless and self-serving. It's a trope that we as a society like to celebrate, admire and role-model. Graciousness is rarely given the spotlight.

When working with founders and leaders on the ground, if I'm honest, nothing can be further from the truth. **Being gracious doesn't mean proceeding without drive, it means proceeding while keeping in mind where you and others have come from and with humble knowledge of where you and others are going.** The founders I've met who practise gratitude regularly are easily the ones who are the most successful and at peace.

I call this grinding with gratitude; getting your head down, working hard, giving it your all, but finding moments to personally reflect on what you are grateful for, and also building systems and language within your business that help your team to do the same.

Robert A Emmons is a professor of psychology at the University of California and the founding editor-in-chief of *The Journal of Positive Psychology*. Through a decade of research and writing, with thousands of people studied from eight years old to eighty, he's found that people who consistently practise gratitude as a learnt behaviour, overwhelmingly have stronger immune systems, are less bothered by aches and pains, and have lower blood pressure. Equally, they exercise more, sleep longer and feel more refreshed when waking. On top of this, they have much higher levels of positive emotions and are more alert and optimistic. They are more helpful, generous, compassionate and forgiving. They also, and perhaps most importantly, feel less lonely and isolated.[12]

Being grateful takes us out of a selfish or self-serving headspace – the headspace which encourages us to think about our own physical, financial or emotional security – and puts us into the headspace which considers others. It helps us gain perspective on how, and the reasons why, others are aiding, and sharing in, our accomplishments.

Scaling a company and leading a team can be one of the most rewarding things we ever do in our lives. We have the opportunity to sculpt and transform not only our own lives, but the lives of those around us – our team, our customers, our families. **As you scale your company you will begin to see other people's lives changing alongside your own.** People will get married, move, have children, take on new responsibilities, adventures and challenges, and, hopefully, find their place within your business in which they can carve out their own path to victory.

The best businesses I've worked with dedicate regular time in their monthly calendars to meet and discuss gratitude for each other, celebrating the various transformations people are living through. When we're gracious, we acknowledge that success isn't a ladder we climb alone. When we speak publicly as a team graciously, we hear others' perspectives of our efforts, and how they have in turn impacted other people. The true sweet spot is when these gracious conversations begin to inform the direction of the business overall, improving team morale and loyalty, and also the bottom line.

Practising gratitude also includes being gracious about failure – this is vital to startup success. You have to create a culture that allows everyone to try new things, some of which won't end up as hoped. Failure is also something that doesn't just happen once, it happens repeatedly. Take for example the lessons in this book. Hopefully, you can start to put them into practice in your own life almost right away, but even if you try to keep them front and centre in your mind, there will be days when you slip. There will be moments when artificial urgency, anxiety, loneliness, shame and your profitable poisons get the better of you. You're human – it will happen. My advice is to resist feeling a sense of frustration. Knowing the lessons and then putting them into practice every day are two very different things, and often we are unpicking unhealthy habits which have taken a lifetime to build. It will take time to unpick them and make new ones. My advice is to be grateful for the times you slip.

In coaching, I call this hitting the rumble strip. When you're driving and you lose concentration you can sometimes hit the section on the edge of the road which alerts you before you continue and hit the barrier. In those moments, we pull back into the lane and avoid the crash. We may also consider what made us drift in the first place and then take action to change things. Perhaps we have a rest or get a coffee at a service station. The same can be said for hitting the rumble strip while building a business. It's only an issue if you crash. If you don't, be grateful for the slip-up and consequent realisation, and for the reminder of the lesson.

Gratitude doesn't care for things that are good or bad; that comes from our own perspective. Gratitude reconnects us to the many reasons why you are striving each day to build a business, and that in turn helps us do so without burning out.

10
Burning Out Is
Often Invisible

Being mindful of your own wellbeing as you forge ahead with your career and protect your business as it scales isn't easy. You're working on something wonderful, something worth investing in, something that has the power to compel other people to join you on your journey. That's infectious. But that experience can so easily push you to, and past, your limits.

How do we know when we've gone from burning out to burnt out? How do we know when we've gone from approaching our limits to exceeding them? **Hitting rock bottom, in reality, is not a single moment but a series of moments. It's spread over months or even years.** It's gradual. It sneaks up on us. Like when you see someone every day and so don't notice subtle changes in their behaviour, appearance or mood.

To you, it seems as if they have always been this way. To you, they never change. It's only when you look back you begin to realise just how much they have shifted from who they once were.

We see people hitting their limits in the news all the time, successful people reaching a point of destruction, we just don't call it out for what it really is. Headline after headline about CEOs, teachers, doctors, lawyers, bankers – all reaching their point of destruction. It's alcoholism, it's drug addiction, it's vandalism, it's shoplifting, it's gambling, it's dangerous driving, it's sex, it's assault, and, at worst, it's suicide.

I'm writing this book because I don't want this to be you. I'm writing this book because no one else seemingly is. I'm writing this book because I hit a limit I didn't know existed until it was too late and it tipped me into self-destruction.

Four years ago I pushed myself too far while scaling my company. I pushed myself so far that I found myself one night driving at 70 mph right towards the edge of a motorway bridge. I didn't want to be in control anymore. I wanted life to take over for a while. I wanted to smash the car off the road with me inside it. Luckily, and thankfully, I managed to stop the car just before I crashed through the barrier, and sat on the side of the road crying.

Since that night, I've done a lot of therapy and a lot of work to understand what was happening to me, and what happens to so many other people reaching for excessive levels of success and ambition while not preserving their wellbeing. I've also made radical changes to my life and my approach to work. I've struggled to speak about it publicly, because there's a lot of shame that comes with telling that story – but I now meet so many others who've experienced similar feelings.

We can create businesses – profitable businesses that can scale to positively impact the lives of others and potentially even sell them for life-changing amounts of money, but we must do so while not destroying ourselves. The key to all of this is building processes and policies which make it easier to check in with one another, and adapt and change when required. The answer is creating companies that listen to their people, build automations to help scale, and give everyone the space to speak honestly.

The rest of this book will focus on the many quick practical hacks I've learnt while starting, scaling and exiting my own business and working alongside other founders, to help you achieve just that.

Resources

Suicide prevention and support

If you've ever had thoughts concerning suicide, you can call 116 123 from any phone, free of charge, day or night, or web chat to trained professionals who can help at www.samaritans.org. There are also tons of resources available through Samaritans that can help you. It's difficult to talk about it. Often, we kid ourselves that there isn't a problem. Let's make one thing clear before we continue any further – the success you want to achieve is entirely possible without the self-destruction that can so often come with it. That is *not* an acceptable trade-off.

Meditation and mindfulness

Meditation and mindfulness have been a huge and invaluable part of my recovery and journey, teaching me how to balance success with peace, and urgency with conscious decision making. So many of us, as founders and leaders, like to live in the future. Our minds consistently go to what is to come rather than what has come about. Mindfulness especially, over time, has been a game-changer in helping bring my mind and body into the present.

I've intentionally held back from including these practices in too much detail in the book. This is because there are so many other books, podcasts and apps that do a great job at signposting and supporting us. Plus, the correct approach for you might not be the approach that has worked for me, it's completely personal.

Some people will respond well to taking time each day to find a moment to practise mindfulness and meditation. The very act of doing nothing at all, and observing that nothingness, constantly bringing ourselves back to the present moment when our minds carry us away in thought, can be one of the hardest things as entrepreneurs to ask our brains to do. It takes work. As comedian and now mental health expert and campaigner Ruby Wax says: 'It's like a sit up.' Wax thinks of mindfulness as more of a workout for the brain. 'No need to go to a gym or lift barbells,' she says. 'All the equipment you'll ever need is in your head and remember your mind is portable – it goes where you go.'[13]

The task at hand with mindfulness is to give your brain an anchor. The best kind of anchor is one of your senses, as this brings you into the present moment and away from your thoughts – the meanderings of our mind which will no doubt pull us in various directions. Many mindfulness practitioners encourage us to draw our awareness to our breath, one of the body's autonomous functions. When we do this, the part of our brain called the insular becomes active, responsible for sensory processing, decision making and motor control. This, in effect, tricks the brain, because it cannot be anxious (for example) and experience a real sensation at the same time. 'It's like a car, you can't put it in two gears. This brings you into the present,' says Wax.

Our brains have been proven to have neuroplasticity – it's possible to train them. Through this process of constantly bringing yourself to the present, your brain will try to distract you away, but through practice, you can rewire your mind to relax your body more intuitively, which helps in those moments, day-to-day, when you start to fill with cortisol, reacting on panic rather than perspective.

If it's not mindfulness and meditation, perhaps it's yoga, or tai chi, or journaling, or even ice baths or cold showers – anything that gets you out of your head and into your body, balancing both your sympathetic and parasympathetic nervous systems. I'd encourage you, alongside putting these into practice, to pick up one of the many wonderful books on mindfulness exercises or download Headspace or Calm; both awesome apps for meditation. Ruby Wax's book *A Mindfulness Guide To Survival* is one of the best I've read.[14]

PART TWO
LEADERSHIP AND CULTURE

11
Sharing Power

Ambition, without management and purpose, is just a burning fire – consuming, growing and likely destroying. Ambition with self-knowledge, humility and direction, on the other hand, is a fire that can change the world – that's the culture you want to build. I see culture, at its heart, as the rulebook that defines the direction that power flows, and the ideal direction for power to flow is from those who have it to those who do not. That's how your culture connects to a genuine purpose of what your business is going to do for others. To build an effective culture, we first need to ask ourselves if we are comfortable holding onto, and then letting go of, power. And if so, what *kind* of power?

To help answer that question, I turn to the work of Henry Timms and Jeremy Heimans, and their book *New Power*.[15] Their research explains there are two types of power, which in turn control cultural movements – old power vs new power. They argue that old styles of control and authority are quickly being eroded by newer structures and systems, which don't have to 'hold on' and 'hoard' power but trust its influence and potential being greater, if shared. This is exemplified in the most successful social crowd-based movements of our generation: BLM, MeToo and Marriage Equality, to name a few.

'Old power works like a currency,' say Timms and Heimans. 'It is held by few; it is closed, inaccessible and leader-driven.' Timms and Heimans suggest that 'new power' works more like a current – it's most useful when it flows and surges. 'The goal with new power is not to hoard it but to channel it,' they say.

When setting the culture for our companies, the concept of 'New Power' is vital. How will your organisation be run for the betterment of all involved, including the owners? This isn't some trendy, moral high ground or altruistic purpose, this is a realistic response to what works best, and what's most sustainable. If you're building for others, for your team, your customers, your clients, your partners, then you're going to build an ecosystem of need, and a reason for your business to continue to exist into the future.

Where this comes into play most is with your hiring strategy. At my own company, we developed an initiative called 'a startup within a startup', which became a fundamental part of our culture and leadership structure. The idea set the expectation that anyone hired at the organisation, at any degree of responsibility or experience, could at some point in their career run their own department, or in fact the whole business. This doesn't sound too dissimilar to traditional businesses' promises of promotions in exchange for loyalty and graft, however our policy had a distinct twist.

When hiring, we explicitly looked for potential entrepreneurs, people who would one day potentially want to run their own business, and then sold them the expectation that anyone who wanted to 'feel like a founder' could do so at our organisation. We looked for ambitious, driven people, who were evangelical about the vision of the company, had proactive ideas about ways they could expand it, and the idea of not just holding onto power, but sharing it, excited them. **On the surface we were running an ad agency, but beneath the surface we were training the leaders of tomorrow. We were looking for our replacements.**

Why did I do this? Because I wanted to build a collective of people who built our company outwards, rather than just upwards. I wanted others to have the opportunities that building equity can bring, and lastly, it just seemed a hell of a lot easier than only hiring people who, on the surface, could be great at their jobs, and who certainly posed little risk to the business, but who lacked entrepreneurial drive.

Now, hiring ambitious and driven people can be risky; many of them may grow tired quickly and wish to leave if they don't see fast results or career progression. To solve this, traditional businesses hire amazing talent and then trade up company perks and training incentives with straight-jacket style commitment agreements that force people to stay: 'Sure, we'll agree to pay for your degree... but you have to then stay with our company for five years.' It's a little gross. The result is traditional businesses setting cultures that reward people for rusting onto their responsibilities. I didn't want to go anywhere near this kind of approach. If ambitious people want career progression and results, let's build a culture that allows them to make that for themselves.

The 'startup within a startup' policy helped with this, together with a couple of rules. Firstly, as promised, at any stage of their employment, any team member that wanted to start a new department in any field they liked, or try a new idea, could do so, as long as it was fully costed. This included a business plan explaining how they would hire to resource their current role (if needed) and then grow their own team. This is something our senior team would offer to help develop alongside them, and could only be progressed when it had senior approval. Secondly, the new department didn't *have* to be anything similar to the others we were currently building, but it did have to feed into the overall social impact mission of our company. Thirdly, and most importantly, we would promise to give the person seeking this opportunity all the time and training required to build their own vision.

The result was a culture that promoted the idea that teaching people how they can grow their own revenue streams is a good thing. Over several years, our organisation would grow outwards, rather than just upwards. We would open new departments, trial international footprints and teams in areas of specialism. It's changed the game and all it took was a little trust and investment in time and guidance. **It came down to our culture, and being open to power flowing, rather than stagnating. It helped encourage each member of our team to further their own self-actualisation.**

One cautionary word on this: an authentic and worthwhile culture that engages people in the 'startup within a startup' opportunity must offer not just autonomy of direction, but also full autonomy of budget. This is crucial, and I've seen half-baked versions of this fail because there was no financial transparency. (There will be more on this in the Operations and Budgets chapter.) At its heart, the people who engage in this kind of policy want to start a business for themselves, so you have to make it real. It can't be superficial, otherwise it's just a fancy title and a nice email footer.

12
Hiring 30/30/30

It goes without saying that you cannot *just* create a business filled to the brim with only potential entrepreneurs – that sounds like an absolute nightmare. You need to bring other types of personalities into the fold, people who complement, balance and progress ideas to fruition. You need people who may seek career progression but don't ever want to run a department, for example, least of all the company. These people are specialists in their field, and while they don't wish to train upwards into management, they do wish to train deeper into their area of expertise. It's your job as a leader to also help these people on their journey.

To ensure a healthy split of personalities across the board, when hiring I recommend the 30:30:30 rule.

Of your hires, 30% should be the entrepreneurs and leaders of tomorrow. You can picture them running departments and maybe even having your job in the future. Your task is to learn what they want to build, and help them build it, retaining them as much as you can.

The next 30% should be those wishing to become specialists in their field, but not move into management. Your job with these folk is to help them deepen their knowledge and understanding, and provide them with exciting opportunities to do that.

The final 30% are those you know are going to leave, after about a year or so. They could be contractors, brought in for short-term projects, seasoned professionals, hired to solve a particular issue or problem, or they could be new graduates who are just getting their foot on the ladder.

The latter (graduates) will hopefully merge into either the 30% group of people you are training to be leaders, or the other 30% group of people you are empowering to deepen their knowledge, but to be real about it, many new graduates who join your company won't wish to be either in a year or so. People change, and often graduates are still working themselves out at this stage; learning 'what work is' while on their first job working for you.

I can hear you asking… 30/30/30? Where's the last 10%? That's your senior management. These could be people progressing from the initial 30% (the leaders) all the way to organisational leadership, or it could be hiring talent that already has the experience from elsewhere. Often in the early stages, startups will not have the cash available to hire people with vast experience of leadership. This is why the strategy I've laid out seeks to train people upwards within your organisation first. 30% grow their own parts of the business outwards and upwards, and within that space created, your second 30% deepen and broaden, utilising the final 30% to strengthen and build. In time, as and when your business begins to flourish, there will be the opportunity and need to hire senior management from outside the organisation. When approaching these kinds of hires, I advise founders to look for people who are a good match to your organisation's core belief system, culture and values.

13
What Are Your Values?

I've lost count of the times I've walked into the corporate headquarters of traditional businesses and
seen words like 'Passion, Innovation, Growth' plas-
tered over the walls of the staff kitchen, usually next
to a sad-looking coffee machine and a kettle that's
seen better days. Your organisation's values shouldn't
be vague business outcomes, and they shouldn't be
untruthful (just look at that kettle!). They should be
about people and beliefs, set from the very beginning
of your company's formation. They should feed into
the very reason you exist as a business, and then be
followed by all team members, not through force, but
through truth and inspiration.

Picture your organisation like a tree. You grow the
branches, the roots, the trunk, and you fill it with

leaves, but if you don't know what kind of fruit it's going to bear, you don't even know if you've planted it in the right place. Getting to grips with the identity of your organisation is crucial to building the right kind of leadership style and culture for your business, because your values are the principal driver for almost all accepted behaviour and decision making.

I refer back to the research of Robert A Emmons, Professor of Psychology at the University of California.[16] When working with businesses and business owners, he asks them to think about describing characters in films or books who are good, and what adjectives come to mind. Perhaps 'brave', 'honest', 'generous' and 'loving'? He then asks them to describe characters who are evil, and what words then come to mind. Perhaps 'selfish', 'hurtful', 'unkind' and 'vengeful'?

Robert's exercise encourages us to notice that every adjective you can think of to describe someone good, describes an act of caring for others, and everything evil, depicts caring for yourself. He argues that good and evil are hardwired into our humanity and therefore into the way we tell stories. Ask yourself, what kind of characteristics do you resemble at work, and what kind of behaviour does your organisation and others you work with traditionally celebrate? Are you the bad guy, and why do you think that is?

At my company, our belief statement was, and still is, **'If you shape history for other people, you end up**

shaping history for yourself'. This was the core idea that started the business; it was my reason for leaving my previous, well-paid job, and seeking investment to start my own agency. I've always believed that if you work to improve the lives of others, work in turn will transform and improve your own life in ways you never thought possible.

Knowing a belief system helps us understand the very nature of an individual or a company – you likely now have a better understanding of why I'm writing this book! Communicating beliefs helps us to determine what kinds of people or organisations are going to have an affinity with us.

Don't hire people who are at odds with your company values, however competent or experienced they are. Ever. Don't hire a financial director who believes authority cannot be challenged, if the very nature of your organisation is to challenge authority. Your cash flow documents won't help you build what you are looking to build. Don't hire a marketing director who doesn't believe that society desperately needs alternative food sources if the reason your business exists is to find them. Your brand won't be truthful to your mission.

14

Make Yourself Dispensable

I was in an interview recently when a journalist asked me to share my best career lesson. I replied by saying, 'Make yourself dispensable,' and they immediately asked back, 'You mean indispensable, right?' 'No, I mean dispensable,' I replied.

The dictionary defines 'dispensable' as being 'able to be replaced or done without; superfluous'. It then continues to list synonyms – 'expendable', 'unnecessary', 'disposable' – none of which I'm sure you'd ever think would be related to entrepreneurship. I bet you didn't think I'd be encouraging you to be any of those things. Why would a leadership book start advising you to focus on becoming, for lack of a better word, irrelevant? I promise you this is not me being sarcastic or smart – it's just the truth.

Do you want your business culture to flourish?

Your job is to work yourself out of a job.

Do you want your team to feel a sense of autonomy and lead with a sense of freedom?

Your job is to work yourself out of a job.

Do you want your company to reach heights of profitability and impact you've only once dreamt about?

Your job is to work yourself out of a job.

Finally, would you like your company to fetch a valuation that is both respectful to its development while also providing you with a firm degree of financial stability?

Then your job is to work yourself out of a job.

It's straightforward but not easy, because it's totally different to what we're told we should do to be successful when working in other people's businesses. If you want your business to be successful without burning yourself out, your culture should enable you to give every job you're doing away to others as you scale your company. If it works the way it should, they in turn should do the same. Let me explain why.

In the early days of building a business, you may not have the means to pay a team of people, but this will change over time. The stronger and more viable the business idea, the shorter this period will be. In the meantime, in that pre-revenue stage, you'll be doing all the jobs required to get the business off the ground. You'll be fundraising in the morning and web designing in the afternoon. You'll be banking the following morning, and then using the rest of your day to write a pitch, complete a job description, work on the brand and meet with a potential investor. It's a lot.

Once you have the means to begin paying people for their time, energy and ideas, your job quickly becomes to find others who can do the things you've been doing better than you have been doing them. Your job also becomes to find others who want the same things as the collective of people you're building, and to teach everyone to also make themselves dispensable. You should continue to do this, again and again, rinse and repeat as your company scales and builds, until the only jobs you are doing are directorial responsibilities, for example tax, and guarding the soul of the organisation, ensuring, like a compass, that all aspects of the team are pointing due north.

That's the job of a founder, and it's hard. We've discussed already how much of a deeply personal journey it can be. There's so much of ourselves that goes into building a business, and with that is our need to be wanted, needed and respected. It's natural. Our ego helps us scale and, at times, that's useful, but your job isn't to build a castle, complete with a throne and a moat, for you to sit in and feel safe. Your job isn't to make yourself so integral to the running of your business that it becomes impossible to peel yourself away from it. Your mission is to build the strongest, most useful and worthwhile organism that you can possibly build. It's an organism that can self-think, self-heal, self-fund and self-grow. It's not a machine, in which cogs can be taken out and identical cogs put in, at will. That's 'old power' thinking. It's an organism that you'll nurture over time and do so by constantly refining it.

This is how the most successful founders approach their businesses. Why? Here's the brutal truth. So many founders create companies based on their belief that they are brilliant, and they might be. They likely are. But no matter how brilliant you are, your job is to successfully grow something that will achieve far bigger things than you could ever do alone, for a longer period than you could ever withstand. It therefore has to be about more than just you. You have to be able to remove yourself from the business, and it still has to operate just as effectively.

This doesn't just mean building your company with and for other people, this means building it with and for other people with the intention of one day letting it thrive without you. It will be very unlikely that your business will find a suitable role for you when it has reached maturity, nor should it. You are a founder, you are a leader, and there will be and should be other exciting opportunities that demand your attention, once that happens. I know this is sometimes difficult to hear. For so long, I pictured myself running my business until I retired. That's a good thing – it means you're passionate about your idea, but in the long term, if you want it to be successful, you have to surround yourself with resources, and very likely even replace yourself.

Where this approach sometimes fails is when founders try to make themselves dispensable too quickly. This isn't something you can rush. It can take years to reach the point where your business is fully ready for its founder to be independent of its day-to-day running. The idea of dispensability, for many, should be an ideal to strive towards. **To do this and to keep doing this for the length of time required, we need to compassionately shift our idea of leadership away from esteem and ego, and towards trusted autonomy and automation.**

15
Automate Everything

In many ways, leadership is looking for efficiencies while balancing the human needs of your team and yourself. As you build your company, your team and your vision, it's worth considering which aspects of your business require direct attention to sustain themselves and which do not. This could include direct attention from you, or from anyone within the organisation. A fairly healthy yet ruthless approach to automation, alongside making yourself dispensable, is vital to growing something that has true value to the world, and to you.

For example, automation can mean hiring someone to do a job you're currently doing and giving them the flexibility and freedom to build upon the foundations you've laid. Automation can also mean using software such as Xero (www.xero.com/uk/) or Quickbooks (https://quickbooks.intuit.com/uk/) to make sure you're seeing the right information about your business at the right time to make informed choices. Automation can even mean looking objectively at your past performance, and making educated guesses about the future to inform whether you hire permanent employees or outsource to freelancers. Each time we must ask ourselves: is this a choice which builds our company to be stronger for the long term? Is this a choice which we will not have to make again? Is this choice going to make our business more independent of us or more dependent on us?

The trick to automation is going all in. The half-in/half-out approach won't cut it. People will feel disempowered, software won't live up to expectations and the business will grind to a halt, awaiting instruction rather than seeking its own solutions. **Automation = autonomy = dependable growth.** Fully trust the choice to automate, give full autonomy in those choices, and build your business in a way which scales independently around you, sustainably for the future.

I say this like it's easy – it isn't. This is extremely hard to do, not just emotionally, but also realistically. It requires trust – something that definitely can't be measured but is certainly immeasurably important to startup success. Like many of the lessons outlined in this chapter, it requires patience and constant refinement. The automations you make in year one aren't going to necessarily do the business any justice by years two or three. Things will constantly need evaluating, updating, tweaking and changing. This is the irony of this lesson – you build for the long term; you try to reach a point that is fully sustainable, knowing in reality that nothing we do in business will be suitable forever. **Everything has to change to remain fit for purpose, relevant and worth our investment.**

A way I like to discuss automation with leaders is to ask them to describe their MVP (minimum viable product). This is a point in time where everything is working to the minimum extent it needs to, on a much smaller scale than it will in years to come. There might be a change required to build up from an MVP, and this is usually likely to be an investment round, but at its bare bones the MVP works. It demonstrates viability.

As we run through their MVP, we discuss their P&L and future projections. I try to get a sense of how the business is performing now compared to how it will perform in a year or so. We then try to get to a place where **each line on the budget remains at roughly the same percentage to total revenue, on a comparative ratio in year one to year three.** By that I mean, if you're spending 20% of your total predictive year-end revenue on marketing that year, you should be looking to spend 20% (or as close to it) of total revenue three years later, otherwise the business isn't pushing towards automation. This could be £5,000 in year one and £50,000 in year three – it doesn't matter.

What matters is that the ratios remain the same, or as close to, to demonstrate that your model is truly an MVP which can automate and scale over time – but not vastly change in its distribution of spend.

It's worth noting here that this doesn't suit every business, and definitely doesn't suit every line on a budget. It's also highly subjective, an ideal to strive towards, not a rule set in stone. For example, a business, if scaling, should be able to grow revenues at a higher percentage rate year on year without all operating expenses increasing as well, and marketing spend should optimise and reduce over time as brand equity and position are built and entrenched. I'll cover this in more detail in the 'Operations and Budgets' chapter.

16

Feedback Loops Vs Echo Chambers

I used to hate feedback. As a creative person at heart, feedback used to etch away at my soul. I'd create something I thought was beautiful, usually a film, as that was my original skillset. It would be finished (or, more accurately, abandoned, because when is creative work ever 'finished'?) and sent out into the world to then be picked apart and dissected, critiqued and destroyed. I used to call it 'killing my babies', as many creative folk say. That was the way I used to see it, at least.

It was only after many years of working across creative projects and beginning to look at my creations as both art and product that I started to realise the more we receive feedback, the more suitable our creation becomes at resonating with the vast array of people we want it to serve. The chip, chip, chipping away isn't just the end of the process; it *is* the process. It was Michelangelo who once said, 'I saw the angel in the marble and carved until I set him free.'

The same can be said for business – the chipping away, the constant refinement, the compassionate sculpting, is the primary job of a leader, and one of the best ways to do this is through working with others to get their thoughts and opinions on your work. Throughout the process of growing my own company and now working alongside many other founders and leaders, I've seen some exceptional examples of feedback being used effectively. In many businesses, though, self-destructive echo chambers still rot away trust in culture and leadership. Why is it that, for some, this goes so wrong?

It comes back to power, and how some believe their role as leader is to control it while others believe we should set it free. New power or old power. **Echo chambers occur at work when individuals either do not allow critique, or set about creating a toxic culture which makes honest feedback difficult to give or receive.** This could be for a number of reasons – perhaps they see critiquing as invalidating their own experience, or they believe that their opinion, being that of the founder, is the most important. Whatever the reason, at its core, echo chambers create a culture that only makes space for one agreed narrative to reverberate through the company. They only let one approved point of view rise to the top and be heard. Echo chambers exist when leaders cannot give up their power and dislike their power being challenged, often stemming from the insecure belief that, if they let it go, it won't come back to them. It will be lost forever. But one of the main reasons for businesses to exist in the first place is to innovate and create change, and usually that only happens when conflicting opinions are allowed to surface and resolve.

Holding onto power isn't the answer to growth and it's certainly not how you build an effective culture, leadership style or team that can sustain wellbeing and scales revenue. A better way to reframe 'critique' is as an opportunity to let go of power and control, for a moment, and empower others. The best businesses I've seen and worked with are the ones that utilise feedback loops that not only allow for opportunities for critique to intersect across the whole company, but also do so transparently and often in a way that's communicated publicly. They create opportunities for their people to engage in debate and critique about almost all areas of the business, including direction, capacity, salary, budgets and operations, etc. They then broadcast this debate internally for everyone to engage with.

Like anything in business, this has to be done in a structured way that both ensures everyone can participate, and that the conversations remain productive and work towards the betterment of the business and its people.

Examples of this include salary-transparency policies (later discussed in the 'Operations and Budgets' chapter), race-equity groups, new business incentive programmes, and team discussions on the direction of the business.

Central to this is hiring people, especially senior staff members, who will call you out on your sh*t, while also actively striving to create a culture that encourages them to do so. This is probably the toughest implementation of feedback loops of them all, because it cuts deep. When you hire and work with people who don't just see their job as affirming your vision and ideas, but independently have their own and challenge yours, it can, at times, certainly cut into your ego. It can make you feel like you're not 'good enough' or that you're inadequate because 'as the boss you should have all the answers'. I say again, your job as a leader is not to pander to your insecurities. Your job as a leader, as a founder, is to create an environment in which others flourish, and guard the integrity of the organisation, ensuring and encouraging everyone within it to point due north. Hiring people who can actively and compassionately critique you, and creating a company where that's permitted and encouraged, doesn't mean you're void of decision making or delegating all responsibility; it means you understand you cannot do it alone. To do anything else may rub on your ego and make you feel more in control, but it will stifle your business in the end.

Do you want to run your business from a place of immobility and ignorance, or awareness and action? The latter will be far more sustainable than the former. Underneath all this is a rule based on the idea that the acquisition of knowledge is never a finite journey, and everyone in the organisation, including the leadership, is learning at all times. Effective feedback loops create self-perpetuating, sustainable cycles, and these cycles, when tried, tested and refined, can be used to scale your business almost on autopilot, by creating opportunities which share autonomy and stop you and others from burning out.

17
Partners Not Clients, Evangelicals Not Employees

When I first started working in advertising and public relations, I was often tasked with calling up journalists and cross-referencing our database with various publications. It was as boring as it sounds, but I did enjoy the prospect of picking up first-hand knowledge of who was working where. I once got on the phone to the news desk at one of the biggest tabloids in the UK, and asked them if a certain journalist was still working there. To my surprise, I was promptly given the helpful advice that, before picking up the phone, I should have perhaps 'tried reading the f**king paper'. Gross. I think this was my first introduction to power dynamics in the workplace – I must have been blissfully unaware beforehand.

In the world of advertising and public relations, much like any workplace or sector, you traditionally have strict hierarchies of power that likely, and far too often, result in those with the least power getting stamped on, overlooked, or, in the worst cases, even mistreated. In many companies, clients regularly have more power and authority than others simply by being 'the client', creating an unhealthy power imbalance built on relationship and influence, rather than experience and skill. I'm sure we can all relate to uneven power structures from our own work experiences. **This doesn't just chip away at people's self-esteem, it chips away at the progression and innovation of the company overall.**

Language plays an influential role in formulating and then reinforcing power in the workplace, so some of the best organisations I've worked with have come up with completely new ways of speaking about those they work for and with. They ask their people to hire evangelicals, not employees, who in turn work with partners, not clients. This straightforward switch of language might sound overly simple and altruistic, but in reality it begins to break down power barriers which hold back organisations and places professionals on an equal footing.

When clients become partners, their wants, needs and experience remain crucially important to the success of a project, as long as they are measured and balanced against the wants, needs and experience of the team being commissioned to work alongside them. When a partner works with an evangelical, not just an employee, you position that person as someone not just completing orders, heeding the needs of someone else without question, but as someone with respected experience and expertise who can add to the success of the project overall.

This approach needs to be catered to every company differently and carefully. A clear line of decision making is important, and balancing power shouldn't erode the understanding that there will always be some within organisations who have more decision-making responsibility than others. But shifting the language, levelling out who is working not *for* but *with* whom, can help to optimise the innovation, growth and performance of the business overall.

18
Decision By Democracy

It's all well and good aiming to even out the power balance within your organisation so that everyone is able to reach for autonomy, both for their jobs and to help build the company. Where this sometimes goes wrong is when the redistribution of power morphs into a hybrid of redistribution of all decision making and redistribution of all risk. Enter decision by democracy – a founder's worst nightmare.

You may think that because democracy works super well in society (well, let's hope we share that opinion), it should also be effective in the workplace – and to a large extent it is. Companies that aren't democratic in their approach are usually s**t to work for. It's therefore important to build businesses that allow for all voices to be heard and discussed, but unlike a true democracy, **these voices are best seen as a referendum rather than a general election**. By this, I mean that listening to the thoughts, ideas and opinions of your team is crucial for guiding the ship, optimising your performance and honing the expertise of your company, but this shouldn't ever replace senior leadership's active involvement in decision making.

Failure is important for growth; you need to try new things that might not work in order to cultivate a company that builds value; the kind of value no one else is building. **A company that decides its entire future on the vote or veto of the entire group will certainly lack a singular, conscious and consistent vision, and I'd put good money on it avoiding risk as well.**

Remember again, your job as founder and a leader is to guard the soul of your organisation. This will mean that, at times, not every choice you make will be popular with the majority. Your job is not to be popular, or to appease or bend to those who shout the loudest. Your job is to listen and then to act.

This is ironic, because so many of us start businesses or work our way into leadership because we want to feel that sense of validation from others, and so many of us build companies where success is so crucial to their team, we don't want to risk disagreeing with our people. To navigate the ship based on this is to end up on the rocks, with no autonomy or sense of individual responsibility when things do run aground.

Democratic systems at work don't always mean democratic decision making. Build consensus, listen to varying opinions, build systems that encourage others to make autonomous decisions, but never let any of this replace true decision making.

19
Ruinous Empathy

I believe empathetic leaders build companies that scale, sustain and potentially sell with the most success. Compassionate and conscious leadership creates cultures that thrive independently of their founders, and grow businesses that, like a tree, flourish in various directions, with deep and stable roots to weather tough times. So why am I about to tell you that too much empathy is bad? Well, too much of anything can be poisonous, and when building your company and your team, there is absolutely such a thing as being *too* empathetic, and I'll explain why.

As you're scaling your business, the impact of most of the choices you make on a day-to-day basis becomes visible almost immediately, or at least fairly quickly, but choosing to be *too* empathetic with your team, and yourself, can result in fundamental problems festering for months, if not years, rotting your business from the inside out. This is when empathy becomes ruinous.

Picture yourself in an appraisal or review meeting with one of your key members of staff; perhaps they are in senior management, or maybe they lead a particular project or department. They are most certainly high performing and have been with your company for some time, showing great loyalty, so you've built a close relationship with them and they have a great reputation with your clients and suppliers. But something has been going wrong, under the surface, and it's becoming an increasing issue.

In this instance, let's say their team has been complaining to you and other co-workers about their behaviour. These complaints have gone through official channels, and now perhaps it's become an open secret that sometimes this member of staff is a completely loose cannon. You've likely become aware for a while that they don't fit your company values, and where once they were great in their role (perhaps they were one of your first hires), now their behaviour is causing far too many problems, affecting team morale and product quality.

You are close to them, though, and you have a great fondness for them, and because of this you also know about their personal issues outside of work, and understand why they are behaving the way they are. You call an appraisal or review meeting to discuss their performance, and they explain in great detail the challenges they are facing outside of work. They speak to such an extent that you find it awkward or even rude to then address the issues and many complaints from other team members. You don't want to rock the boat further and they are still delivering some good results, so you choose to avoid the subject altogether.

Months go by, and by now the problems with product quality and team morale have become overwhelming. Staff turnover has gone through the roof, and this individual can't seem to hold onto a team for longer than a few months. You call another meeting with them, this time a formal disciplinary, and explain that things are at breaking point and their behaviour has led you to feel like you need to dismiss them.

Herein lies the problem – they didn't know there was an issue and they are ultimately bamboozled by your news. Due to your hesitancy, they were completely unaware of the concerns you have had for months, maybe even years, and, knowing their job is now on the line, they end up handing in their notice, at best, or at worst, challenging you with legal proceedings.

This is ruinous empathy at work. **Often, especially as founders, we build close and trusted relationships, even friendships, with those we employ, and we desperately want them to feel good about working**

at our company. Many founders, as I've already discussed, found companies through loneliness or trauma, so having close relationships with people at work and being liked by them is important. Perhaps these people are integral to the running of a particular department and without them the company would suffer? Perhaps they have been a trusted confidant over the years, helping you through tough times as your business has scaled? There can be 101 reasons why we're hesitant to discuss critical feedback with someone, and why we choose to be more empathetic with them than assertive, but rest assured, the empathy you are displaying in these instances is ruinous.

More often than not, ruinous empathy is extremely subtle. It can be in response to a great many issues with someone's performance far less severe than emotional outbursts and low team morale. It could be consistently under-acknowledging someone who repeatedly takes too much time delivering projects, or perhaps someone frequently delivering substandard work. Whatever the reason, being too empathetic with your team at a time when you need to be gracefully guiding and coaching them is a loss of leadership, and, furthermore, a deficiency in meeting their trust in you. It's actually a collapse of true compassion, because in these moments we have the opportunity to step up and help them; to shepherd them and optimise their performance and success. However close you are to your team, they are expecting you to be open and honest with them, so they have time to address issues and have the opportunity to improve and learn.

It's a delicate symmetry to sustain, and at times it's incredibly tricky to strike the right balance, but remember: you are the protector of your team's well-being and success. It's your job to guide them, and to know them, however difficult that may be at times, and they will be thankful for it, if you truly have their best interests at heart.

In these moments it's good practice to ask yourself what kind of leader you want to be – one that isn't fearful to graciously guide, or one that's gentle with the truth in response to fear and a desire to appease? Your answer to that question is central to your response to ruinous empathy, and how you build a successful company without burning yourself out or those around you.

20
Plan Through Perspective, Not Preoccupation

When I was young, I developed a hypervigilance around money, safety and security. Through understanding my own profitable poisons, I now know that these traits helped me build a successful business, and I've learnt to let go of the negative emotions and triggers which have long been associated with these behaviours. This has taken many years of work, with specialists, therapists and friends – and what's left is someone who is now able to dip into these behaviours, use them, help others with them, without risking feelings of anxiety and depression.

Many founders have a form of hypervigilance, which makes them exceptional at their job. As we've discussed, the trick is first to understand where these behaviours come from, and then to implement them consciously, and with compassion.

One such hypervigilance I come across often when coaching founders is one directed towards the future. Of course, what is to come in each of our futures is largely uncontrollable – but not completely. **Many founders make it their mission to control the future, by assessing many possible outcomes at once, making plans for each eventuality.** This is a wonderfully powerful behaviour to practise when building a business, if approached in a conscious way. Although it's impossible to control every future occurrence or situation, planning for the most probable outcomes helps us stay one step ahead and helps us point our companies due north. A pilot will make contingency plans for bad weather, equipment failure, etc, and, in the same way, so should a founder and their senior leadership team.

It's important that throughout this process of planning, we focus on planning with perspective, and not with preoccupation. I've come across founders who meticulously prepare for eventualities which are not only highly unlikely but also highly traumatic. They think about what they would do if their company were to go bankrupt, for example, or if all team members quit at exactly the same time. When we plan for possible outcomes and make decisions based on these assumptions, there is a part of our brains and our bodies that actually 'lives out' these eventualities, especially if we're driven to make decisions based on empathy. Mix in a healthy dose of insomnia, and you've got a sleep-deprived leader worrying about dire situations that have close to zero chance of happening.

The power you must find is to learn to make decisions based on perception and perspective. **The best indicator of future events is past events, and the best indicator of future behaviour is past behaviour.** As you grow your business, set about looking for trends that can help you and your team plan for the future. This could be a time every year, exactly in the same period, when sales dip, for example. By developing a sense of perspective, we can interpret data as it appears in a more conscious and accurate way, refining our resilience.

The hard thing to do in these instances, however, is to fight the urge to act on impulse when things aren't working out as planned. When we see something happen in our business, something we have perhaps prepared for but isn't quite working out the way we thought or hoped, the chances are we want to hop right on those issues and quash them. We want to fix them quickly and get back on track. But making choices based on perspective is a calm, quiet and gentle experience – it isn't quick or rash and is rarely urgent.

I had a great boss who once told me that you should be the last person in the room to speak if you are the leader. There should be systems of automations and autonomous team members in place, ready to solve issues independently, without your involvement. If they need nudging towards 'true-north' at times, do so gently, but only after everyone else has had their moment to speak. Challenging times are a great test to understand if your business is truly working; if the automations and systems you've put in place really are fit for purpose. It's easy to create processes when times are good, when things are working out as expected – it's much harder to put those automations to the test, to truly trust and rely on the autonomy of your team, when things are happening that haven't been planned for.

When we give advice as leaders, or need to make choices ourselves, we should make it clear that any decision should be taken only when conflicting advice has been given, when those making decisions have the full breadth of perspective possible. This is why I like to stack my boards with people who think differently to one another – only through sifting through different perspectives are you able to reach the most viable and stable plan. I've actually been known to take on the role of devil's advocate in senior leadership meetings, sometimes to the annoyance of my team! I'll challenge ideas or give conflicting advice – not because I want to stress the process, but because I want to stress-test the autonomy of the company. There is *never* one right answer, and often two completely different points of view are actually both correct.

As a founder, it's sometimes your responsibility to seek out and give conflicting advice and allow your team to use their best judgement to make the right decisions. This is how you inspire independent thinkers. If they choose a path which leads to a failure, everyone has learnt a lesson, and the business has built a stronger automation and is now optimised better for the future.

Decision making of any kind can, at times, lead to cyclic thinking or indecision. An exercise I often coach to combat this is called 'walking through a door'. It's as simple as it sounds. When you need to make a difficult decision, and perhaps you're trapped in a moment of cyclic thinking, simply stand before a door (it could be any door in your home or office) and say to yourself, 'this door is my decision. When I walk through it the decision will have been made, and no further thinking (or overthinking) is going to change it.' Then… you wait… as long as it takes, and only when you're ready to make that promise to yourself should you walk through the door.

It's odd, but the physicality of this exercise, of visualising a decision as a door and making the choice to walk through it when we are ready, really helps to let go of overthinking and trust that your judgement is based on perspective, not preoccupation. There's actually a cool bit of science to back it up. Research by Radvansky and Copeland in 2006 showed that our brains react to 'thresholds' to new environments, like doors, by filing information and memories away.[17] It's like our minds see doorways as 'save points'. It's also why sometimes you walk into a room and forget why you came in! Spatial changes to different locations act as boundary markers to segment continuous information. Next time you're hit with a moment of indecision, go find a door.

21
Embrace Courage

While scaling our businesses, it's vital that we understand what powers us but also what holds us back. Often, as we've discussed, there can be fundamental aspects of our personality which propel us to begin building a company, which can in turn lead us to burning out or feeling overwhelmed. As we progress, being conscious of this self-reflection, we must try at the same time to balance this with a sense of pushing forwards, and finding the courage to step into ourselves – the person we want to be, and the person our company needs us to be. For instance, knowing you are perhaps powering aspects of your business through anxiety or artificial urgency shouldn't be a reason to stop powering it forwards. Far from it. It should be the fuel required to proceed consciously, in a more healthy, sustainable way. It takes courage to not hold back once you have done the inner work.

In the same way, the way we choose to communicate with others at work, especially in the face of adversity, also takes courage. I'd bet good money on you having heard the phrase 'see no evil, hear no evil, speak no evil'. Often depicted together as three wise monkeys, one covering their eyes, the next covering their ears, and the last covering their mouth, the phrase originated as an ancient Japanese proverb. It was made popular in the seventeenth century as a pictorial Shinto maxim, carved in the famous Tōshō-gū shrine in Nikkō, Japan. In Buddhist belief, the proverb refers to not dwelling on negative thoughts – an important lesson when scaling a business. Important for founders is the proverb's perhaps more modern meaning – referencing a code of silence, or not calling out truth to power. To me, this acts as a warning.

As founders, we must avoid remaining silent when required to speak up, even if it's uncomfortable or awkward. We must, when required, **embrace the courage to say the unsayable**, while remaining mindful and conscious of other people's points of view.

There will be moments when those around you hold back, leaning away from addressing fundamental issues for fear of confrontation or soured relationships, but the guardianship of your organisation's soul requires you to always be the person to speak up when it's needed. Perhaps someone in the company, even your investor, for instance, is influencing decisions that are causing your business to stray from its sole purpose? Perhaps partners and clients you are working with are consistently making your team feel inferior or undervalued? Or maybe you want to address your *own* choices or behaviour as problematic? It takes guts to speak up, especially to those who traditionally hold more power over us than most, but very few others will speak for you, nor should they.

If you are to embrace the courage to say the unsayable, it's crucial to remain conscious and compassionate, while also being extremely considerate of the language you choose to use. Try inserting words into your sentences which allude to the possibility of debate, and at the same time, reject words that limit or downplay your request. For example, instead of saying, 'I'm only concerned about the way our people are being underpaid while working on this project', try switching it up to, 'I'm concerned about the way our people are perhaps being underpaid while working on this project'. It's *very* subtle, and some may even say unimportant or trivial, but removing the words 'only' or 'just' and inserting the word 'perhaps' makes a huge difference to how it's received.

We must never be convinced that our position is 100% correct. In business, there's always room for interpretation. Try using words such as 'perhaps', 'maybe' or 'possibly' to open up the conversation to discussion.

In the same way, avoid using words like 'just', 'only' or 'simply', which soften or lessen your argument. A little bit of humility goes a long way.

The truth is, increasingly, the way we communicate as leaders is often all our people have to judge us on. The bigger your company gets, the more digital and remote it becomes, the less direct interaction people will have with you. Therefore, what we say and how we say it, as leaders, directly affects how we make people feel. We set the culture, especially with the written word – which now lives forever and can be searched, reviewed and even published, across multiple platforms.

Semantics are crucial. Firstly, they will help you to avoid censoring yourself in the face of adversity. Secondly, they will safeguard the mutual respect of your leadership. Lastly, they will assure that those around you understand it's sometimes ok to say things that are uncomfortable.

22
You Work For Them

Your leadership will be remembered for the extent you are able to balance both guarding the soul of your organisation with the compassion required to look out for and support your team. Often, when we become 'the boss' we can misunderstand that the people we hire are working 'for' us. My approach has always been the reverse of that. I keep in mind at all times that I am working 'for' them.

Our job as founder, as leader, is to look out for and hire exceptional people, and then be hypervigilant to their needs and wants. Our role is to help accelerate their passions and desires to further their own careers, to fulfil the impact they are looking to make on the world, and to help them use our business as a vehicle to do that. Our company helps shape their lives, and in return they help shape our business. In this sense, the direction our company takes shouldn't be set in stone at the start of each year, remaining steadfast and unchanged. To do this would be confusing 'direction' with 'purpose'. The purpose of our company and its mission should remain largely fixed, but its direction should ideally always remain as fluid as possible.

If you can genuinely and deeply understand the motivations of your team, and you're willing to compassionately meet people where they are at, not where you want them to be, you can begin to shape the culture of your company and your leadership style in a way which doesn't wound the wellbeing of you or your team, but instead strengthens it. As a founder, as a visionary, it's easy to get lost in our future hopes and ambitions for people's trajectory, and therefore the trajectory of your business, but the future isn't certain.

Instead, try to keep in mind that you work for them, and while you can encourage and guide them, **leadership works best not by pulling from the front (fending off any obstacles) or pushing from the back (whipping people into shape) but by standing alongside and shepherding, nurturing and, above all, respecting**. If you have the right people around you, you must do for them what they deserve, which is to provide them with the space they need to thrive. Once you can do this, your business will begin to scale organically and autonomously – the sweet spot we're forever aiming for.

PART THREE

PITCHING YOUR STARTUP TO CLIENTS, CUSTOMERS AND INVESTORS

23
Investing In You

Pitching: putting yourself out into the world with your best foot forward and asking for what you need. Whether you're looking for new investors or new clients, building your network and pipeline of revenue is vital. Without that, there's no business. Obviously stated.

What's not so obvious is why people will invest in your business. Knowing this is pivotal to the pitching process. They'll invest their time, their energy or their cash. This can be for a number of reasons, one of the most frequent of which, and ironically most frequently overlooked, is *you*. You are the backbone of your business, your identity is so closely interwoven with your company's that some days it would be hard to tell you apart, no doubt. That means we have to make sure you're comfortable talking about yourself without modesty, without ego and with authenticity, as quickly as possible.

I used to train individuals for media interviews. During the process, we'd select the types of outlets clients would like to appear on, or the types of stories that would best suit their experience. Together, we would chip away at their personas, fine-tune their personal brand and rehearse their key messages, all to create a sellable product. None of this was inauthentic. We weren't making anything up, and that's the key point – we were simply making the most of the parts of them that were most investible to their target audience.

Much like in the news, when we're pitching a business for new investors or new clients, we're selling a story, and the story is *you*. Your business may change its direction several times during the course of a vested interest, but what's most likely not going to change is the reason why you are building it. What is your *why*?

The trick is to start seeing yourself as a potential R&D project for your investors. The question then becomes not how much you require to build your business, but instead, **how much do you need to unlock the time for you to realise the potential of their investment**? Early-stage investors are getting in at a time when the track isn't built and the train barely has wheels. What they are punting their bets on is the driver. And that's ok. That's expected. What they are getting in return for this risk are sizable tax discounts (explained later) and a hefty discount on the share price, should you rocket in size and value to where everyone hopes.

With this in mind, let's make sure we can get you to a place where you know *who* you are and *why* you want success. Moreover, let's encourage you to talk competently and without embellishment about why and how you are able to build your company for the long haul, weathering the inevitable storms that will arise. The best kind of investors are betting on those storms and your ability to be honest about figuring them out, not by being immune to them.

Type 'entrepreneur' into LinkedIn or Instagram and get ready to be bombarded with glossy shots of supercars, private jets and promises of making five-figure sums every month for the rest of your life. When we engage with this type of content we bear witness to, at best, inauthentic inflations of ego, and at worst, age-old claims of storm immunity. Both are highly destructive to our wellbeing and self-esteem, because they just aren't true. This is 'entrepreneurship on steroids'. It is a symptom of the simple yet widely accepted mantra that we all must 'fake it till we make it', and that the only way we should compete is with lies and a highlights reel.

While social media provides ever-more accessible comparisons to the Bezos and Musks of the world, we've seemingly inherited a hive-minded toxic belief that every entrepreneur should be killing it. This belief has singlehandedly perverted and twisted the idea of business ownership into something which isn't just inauthentic, or even wildly unattainable but, I believe, highly detrimental to our wellbeing. **How can we ever compete in a system, once designed for healthy competition, which now stacks the odds so far from our favour?** I've spoken to small startup owners who stay up at night worried about how they can beat Amazon to the top spot, while forgetting that the real glory is in carving out their own marketplace, within their own authentic and achievable parameters.

Now, I'm not saying don't dream big. Dream *big*. That's your job as the founder. There's a lot to be said about stepping up and pitching using larger-than-life language that paints a perfect picture of the future, to help you navigate that path with confidence. I told people for years that I was building the most groundbreaking digital agency the world had ever seen. It took me far too long to realise what truly matters was not impacting the lives of *every* human on Earth, but to first genuinely impact the lives of the people I was already engaging with. Start from there. Pitch from there.

The truth is, 'fake it till you make it' is an illusion. It's... fake. It's not real. Believe it for a little, and you can use it to push you forward; believe it for too long and you risk becoming separated from the reality of how your business is really performing, or why it even exists. **Your job when pitching is to sell the vision without peddling an illusion; story-tell the future, but keep it real.**

24

Inauthentic Pitches Lead To Inauthentic Or Badly-Suited Investors

Not being yourself in a pitch, or selling an idea you know is untrue, doesn't just set you and your team up for failure – for that huge fall from grace – it most likely leads you to making deals with investors who don't know the real you. Great – you've got your money, but it came at a hefty price. You've now sold out to someone who isn't a match. They don't know the real reasons why you're starting your company, why you want to build what you're building, and, most of all, they don't understand the speed at which you want to build it. This risks them pushing you to accelerate to an unsustainable level of growth based on miscommunicated expectations of when they can realise the potential of their investment.

Yes, you are investible – but not investible to anyone and everyone. You have to find your kind of people. You want to find smart money; people who have the cash to prop up your research and development, but who also have the relevant experience and knowledge to help you along the way. If you can truly be yourself when pitching, without modesty and with honesty, you will find people who share your vision and want to help make it happen, but who also compassionately understand where you're at today. If done right, this can be a relationship that lasts decades, even after the investor has potentially sold their shares and moved on to pastures new.

The problem is, **as founders, many of us are people who live in the future**. We have a vision of the world, often inspired by overcoming trauma and injustice in our own lives, and we see endless potential for betterment. That's wonderful. It's enchanting. It's so much more interesting than where we currently are when pitching to investors. And therein lies the problem.

The trick is learning that where you are right now, at whatever stage of the journey you're at, is just as good, just as pitchable and just as investible, as the vision of where you hope to be. Crucially, it's vitally important your authentic self is part of your pitch, so you begin to do business with people who understand your drivers and your triggers, and can help you reach a shared goal. To do this, we need only help you find your authentic story and help you make it a story worth telling, to the right people.

EXERCISE – THE STORY OF SELF

- Sit in a circle with your team and each hold a piece of paper and a pen.
- Individually write down your story of self; the important stages of your life-journey that have led you to being the person you are today. The more authentic and open you can be, the better, but no one should be encouraged to share private details they don't wish to.
- Split into smaller groups of 2–3 people, and begin sharing your stories with each other, in turn. Those listening should be encouraged to ask questions and start open discussions with those sharing.

The entire team should then regroup, and if they feel willing, people should be encouraged to share the details of what they learnt during the breakout sessions and continue to discuss these themes as a larger group. They could perhaps begin to discuss how the stories were similar and how perhaps they tie into the overall mission of the organisation.

This exercise works best when everyone participates, from CEO to apprentice. What you will find is that, despite our differences, we are far more alike than we are dissimilar. It's good for the team to truly understand who they are working alongside each day, but equally, as founders and leaders, it's good for us to uncover perhaps fundamental experiences we've been through that have driven our choices. What is the life experience you are responding to by starting your company? How can this story form part of your pitch, part of your organisation's story? And how can it, in turn, make you more investible to the right kind of people?

25

Make The Ask And
Then Shut Up

People often think pitching is a purely verbal sport... it isn't. Far from it. When we're pitching, it's important to utilise both speech and silence. This fine balance will help you navigate the conversation, and help transform it into a two-way conversation, not a one-way broadcast.

One of the finest pieces of pitching advice I was ever given is to 'make the ask – and then shut up'. Often, when it comes to asking for money and discussing budgets, due to our own insecurities, we feel the need to speak too much, repeating unnecessary things or filling the space when silence creeps in. I'm here to tell you, **resist the urge to fill the silence when pitching** – just ask for what you need, state the value of the work, and then let the silence do the talking.

It's actually *extremely* tricky to do. Try asking a friend to donate to a charity, for instance. You perhaps explain what the charity does, its past success, why the leadership is great and why the organisation exists. You perhaps mention the value most people have given in donations, providing a ballpark figure. You then make the ask for them to donate, and what comes next is silence. Thinking time. You try leaving it longer than five seconds without speaking. It's tricky, especially if you're an empathetic person.

Try to always end your budget slide with a question, because questions entice answers; they ask for the silence to be filled. In fact, when pitching to a client or investor, what they say immediately after you've presented the budgets is perhaps the *most* valuable insight you will get from them during the whole pitch. What they say to fill that silence will hint not just at their interest, but also their willingness or ability to invest at the speed you're looking for, and that's the vital information you need to get clarity on as quickly as possible.

26
Affect The Energy In The Room

The human body is like a tuning fork to its environment. When pitching, it's your responsibility to be the one affecting the energy in the room. When people do this well, you can feel it. Ever genuinely smiled during a meeting or belly-laughed out loud? I don't mean that corporate bulls**t laugh that makes everyone feel validated, I mean *really* laughed?

There is a well-known saying: 'People will forget what you said, people will forget what you did, but people will never forget how you made them feel.'[18] Genuinely change the energy in the room and you will get their attention. How do you do this?

Step one: be human. Be relatable. Be *you*. Be the honest version of yourself you've refined for this audience.

Most importantly, genuinely look to discover what it is people want from you, and then look for ways that you can give them that. The business of trade goes on long before someone begins officially 'trading' with you. During the pitching stage, you're trading emotions, feelings, relationships, networks, and competing for a genuine need that the other person has. To do that well, you have to figure out what makes them tick and what they want. Could it be a promotion from their boss? If they are a potential investor, could it be a powerful new addition to their portfolio they can show their friends? Do they want to win awards? Do they want a legacy for their children? What do they want? The first few meetings with an investor or prospective client are chances to learn these crucial nuggets of information. A healthy Instagram or Facebook stalk might also help! (But you didn't hear that from me.)

Step two is to get to the bottom of why they want it and how you can help them. To do this, you just have to be open and honest about why you're doing what you're doing. The more honest you can be the better, because that energy is infectious and it will be mirrored. Don't be afraid of getting vulnerable.

In his book *Lost Connections*, Johann Hari explains the findings of researcher John Cacioppo, who studied building meaningful relationships and overcoming loneliness.[19] He explains that to build a worthwhile connection you 'need to feel like you are sharing something with the other person which is meaningful to *both* of you. You have to be in it together – and "it" can be anything that you both think has meaning and value.' It's not enough to know what they want, it's not enough to be able to just broadcast what you can offer – you both have to want the same thing; you have to both want to help each other, genuinely. That's a successful pitch.

Another great way to affect the energy in the room is with a skill I like to call 'language remixing'. If you talk like an investor, an investor is far more likely to take you seriously. So don't just know your SEIS from your EIS (we'll get to this a little later), but listen actively and intently to the way they phrase things. This works exceptionally well with prospective clients, also. Listen to how people speak and begin to use their language back at them. Remix it. The best salespeople I've ever met do this without even thinking. It shows you're listening, and the best way to get someone to pay attention is to speak in a manner they most recognise.

This includes also getting clued up on the acceptable narratives of the day. What are the friends and contacts of your potential investor or client talking about? What's happening in the news and current events that would most concern them? Start and end your meetings with active discussions about these topics, and begin to not just affect the energy in the room, but also start to truly **understand whether they respond to and match that energy, and if so, whether they are the right investor or client for you.**

27
Keep It Punchy

It's often hard to focus on all of these tactics at once, alongside actually pitching a lot of information in a short amount of time. The suggested length of initial pitches in most coaching workshops is now around five minutes, and follow-up pitches are around only half an hour. That's not long at all, and attention spans are seemingly getting shorter and shorter. There are two easy ways to ensure you're performing at your best when pitching and keeping things punchy.

The first is thinking of a pitch as theatre. Every performance needs its set, cast and plot. When you're watching a performance, everything should point your attention to the actors, helping the audience become immersed in the story and forget they are in a theatre entirely. The last thing you want to watch is an actor badly reading from an autocue. It ruins the belief. With this in mind, your presentation slides should be a prop not a prompt, using text sparingly, relying mainly on images and graphs, adding colour, context and illustration. Of course, a more detailed version should be made available for email follow-ups, a vital stage of the process.

Alongside theatre, we can also take inspiration from the news. This is a tactic I picked up while training as a journalist in my early years. A newsreader should tell you the headline in seven words or less, with detail then following: who, what, where, when and why. 'How' the story has occurred then features afterwards. Newsreaders are also accompanied by brief text on screen, with images, video and graphics. These are refined tactics, tried-and-tested methods that gather the most amount of attention and understanding in the shortest time possible. Embody them. Copy them. Use them to your advantage. And, like any performer, rehearse, rehearse, rehearse.

28
Spin Your Weaknesses

A tactic I like to teach when coaching founders is to consciously monitor and respond to the reasons why a potential investor or client wouldn't choose them. I ask them to write down all the possible reasons why they might lose the pitch and what negative assumptions the investor or client may harbour about them. This is before the meeting goes ahead. It might sound harsh, but if you're not thinking about your weaknesses, the person you are pitching to sure will be, and we want to give them no excuses to not work with you. Plus, as they say, self-awareness is sexy.

As a founder, thinking about our weaknesses isn't something we usually like to consider too often. It creates feelings of wanting to solve our issues rather than just owning them. It kicks in that negative self-monologue and only adds to the never-ending list of to-dos. At pitch stage, there will always be reasons for investors or clients not to pick you, however advanced your company becomes. The task at hand is to get ahead of them. The task at hand is to understand your barriers to growth.

These weaknesses could be anything: lack of experience, team size, funding, insight, diversity, industry clout, network; the list goes on and on. Before every pitch, take the time as a team to discuss yours. The list will be different for each potential investor or client, so it's something you'll need to revisit every time. Once you have your list, next to each point, **think about why each weakness actually works in your favour.** For example, a lack of experience in the sector makes you potentially innovative and creative, more likely to break the mould. A small team size makes you adaptable, able to be an extension of the client's team and also give them the full weight of the company's support, including the founder – something a client wouldn't get if they chose a bigger company.

Thinking ahead of time about how each of your 'weaknesses' could actually help the person you are pitching to demonstrates self-awareness, authenticity and maturity; winning attributes for pitches and great relationship builders.

29
Communicate Urgency

Too often, urgency is something that holds us back from reaching our potential as founders and leaders; a thorn in our side or a distraction that ends up being our Achilles' heel. When it comes to pitching, however, urgency is actually our friend, as long as it's authentic.

When you pitch to an investor or prospective client, it's worthwhile giving them a deadline to create a sense of urgency. If the investment round closes in X days, for example, or there are only Y shares left available in the investment pool, 'with spaces filling up fast', it creates a sense of needing to act now or risk missing out.

Where this goes wrong is when founders lie or when the deadlines shift. It sets the ground for some dodgy relationships and some fairly difficult and avoidable conversations. Where I've seen it done well is during email marketing which funnels people to pitch meetings.

> '1,200 people have joined our crowdfunding campaign. We're oversubscribed and have opened a further stretch goal that has to close by midnight on Sunday. Interested in chatting more? Get in touch.'

I've also seen it work well as a small mention at the start of the pitch.

> 'How's your morning been? We decided to pack in three other investor meetings this morning back-to-back and everyone wants follow-up chats.'

Communicating urgency in this way can nudge people who are close to committing but who are not yet convinced over the finish line.

30
Automate Clarity

Many of the lessons in this book are about balancing the extent to which we can build our businesses with authenticity, while also setting up boundaries and structures that automate their growth and harness our time. This is the key to working without wounding our wellbeing. One aspect of this is to **automate who gets the most of your attention and why**.

Getting clarity on whether an investor or client is interested in your company and what their potential timeline would be are core parts of that first meeting. With time being your most valuable resource as a founder, getting these answers helps to understand more deeply the motivations of those you meet and where your time should be best spent. The next step is to automate this need for clarity, and pull it into an easy, quick-reference matrix, allowing you to spend your time where it's most likely to bring about a win, and help you scale sustainably without burning out.

Example matrix

Status	Cold	Neutral	Warm	Hot
Detail	Not interested right now	New prospect	Keen to work together	Keen to begin work together
Action to be taken	Disregard – add to email database	Get a meeting booked in	Get approval on a proposal	Get signed contract
	Person A	Person B	Person C	Person D
	Person E	Person F	Person G	
	Person H	Person I	Person J	
	Person K	Person L		
	Person M			

Step one is to build out a structure of columns representing how close the person is to working or investing in your company. This can range from 'they aren't interested' through to 'they want to know more' through to 'they are inches from signing'. I've also seen it done using colours or heat, to be more objective. 'Red' or 'Freezing' means they aren't interested, 'Green' and 'Boiling Hot' means they are ready to sign.

Step two is to structure an action point for each column, and a purpose for each meeting that's due to happen. This action point should signpost people from one category to the next. For example, the first email is to book the first meeting, and that's its sole purpose. The first meeting is to obtain information about what they want, what their budget is and when they might be interested in working together. The second meeting is there to give a deeper understanding of these points, perhaps with you reflecting on their original feedback. The structure will be different depending on whether you're talking to an investor, a partner, a client or a customer, so make these as specific as possible for the types of meetings you take.

Step three is to place your contacts on this matrix, considering how close you feel they are to working with you or investing in your company. Then, once a week – usually on a Tuesday because Mondays are hell on Earth for most people's inboxes – you follow up with everyone on your matrix with the aim of moving them closer to the top of the funnel. These email follow-ups can be pre-written with space for personalisation to help you get through it quickly. They can be detailed or as simple as, 'Hey Anika, Just following up to get something in the diary this week or next?' Regardless of length, each email should finish with a question and a deadline.

Step four is to create more bespoke communication for those near the top of the chain, the ones most likely to be worth your time and effort. This might be weekly or fortnightly phone calls, feedback sessions, early-stage mock-ups or discussions – whatever they need, and most importantly you need to make sure that working together is likely to be a success for both parties.

Now, automating clarity can all seem a little soulless, yes, and that's something I ask founders to wrestle with in their own way as they adopt this model. Automating anything, including the clarity of your pipeline, should help you have time to make better, more human decisions, and that shouldn't result in the process feeling robotic or impersonal. It has to work for you and the people you work with, because pretty soon you'll be finding yourself rolling out this automation to other members of your team, empowering them to make their own choices about where to place people on the matrix, and how they get them closer to the goal of working together.

31
Become Rejection Immune

If you automate clarity, you're going to receive rejection in bucket loads. Why? People shy away from confrontation. **The more you nudge people for clarity, the more you will get negative responses – the type of responses that folk may have otherwise kept to themselves if they hadn't been chased.** Haven't heard back yet from a prospect? They might be busy or they might be avoiding telling you they aren't interested. If you don't know where they stand, you don't know how much time to dedicate to them. In the world of seeking clarity, 'no' is as useful an answer as 'yes' – although let's face it, 'yes' is a whole lot better!

In the early years of scaling my business, each time I got a 'no' from a potential investor or client (and there were many) it would crush me. The weight of the organisation I was building, and the burden of its need for cash flow, would be a physical pain on my shoulders. However, **before long I started to realise that rather than focusing on 'no' as a negative, I should instead be grateful for the clarity**. This isn't just because I then knew where I stood with that prospect, but, over time, our company began to get a more detailed picture from the data of what types of organisations and individuals were most interested in us. We began to understand more about what people found most rewarding in our pitches, and, in turn, how we could increase the win-rate tenfold. A 'no' really was as valuable as a yes. It helped us refine our offering.

32
Emote, Educate, Action

Pitching doesn't start and stop at the pitch. Once you're finally pitching to someone, it's likely they have already engaged with something you have written, made or coded at least twenty times. The founders I see who do this well understand that everything that surrounds them (usually digital) is architecture designed to pull in like-minded people. Everything has a purpose, from the website to the business card. Everything has to masterfully do its job of nudging someone up a commitment curve.

What's the best way to pull in like-minded people? Emotion. It touches the heart, lending itself to lived experience, to nostalgia, and to feelings of familiarity. I coach a technique called 'Emote, educate, action' with founders and leaders. This is the idea that all outward communications that first reach an individual need to be emotional. The end result of the strategy could be any action – investment, donation, partnership, anything. Too often, I see organisations jumping straight to education in their communications, because, frankly, it's easier. But people scrolling on social media or milling around at a networking event aren't looking to be educated, at least not most of the time. **They are looking to be entertained. They are looking to be enchanted.** They are looking for a distraction that makes them feel something, and it's your job to give that to them. Education is boring. People may say they want to learn something, but most of the time they don't. Certainly not at first. Not until they trust you as a *credible* source.

Concentrate on emotionally engaging the people you are looking to bring into your inner circle. Want a potential investor to stop scrolling and pay attention to your startup? Create something meaningful, emotive and, most importantly, relevant to their lived experience, that makes them feel something. Want to get the attention of a potential new client at a networking event? Start the conversation by asking them about their lives. Don't be inauthentic; genuinely listen and talk about things occurring in your own life that are similar.

Focusing on emotion first has led to some fascinating conversations. I once had a half-hour discussion with a former UN Secretary General about navigating mortgage rates and gearing up my credit rating to buy my first apartment. He genuinely wanted to help me out and I think he also welcomed a discussion which was completely different to the usual, 'educational' approved narratives that most people discuss at such events – 'Wasn't the presentation wonderful? What are your team working on at the moment?' Ugh. Dull. You can get to that eventually. First – **build a human connection.** Build some emotion.

That also means the story you tell about yourself and your business has to be an emotional story worth telling. In short, it cannot be boring. The most compelling founders and leaders I've worked with are expert storytellers, casting their organisation as the protagonist to all who will listen.

What comes next? Your website is your digital shop window, so it should not only story-tell where you are right now, it should also sell where you are going. You have to be seen as a safe, stable and investible pair of hands, and in this sense, your website must dispel any feelings of risk the audience may feel towards your brand. The first thing visitors should see should be emotive; don't jump straight to education. Start with why you exist, and then begin to slowly educate. The ask for an action – which at this stage is usually to set up a meeting – should be at both the top of the website and the bottom. It should ideally also be a button which follows the visitor all the way down as they scroll through. **Emote, educate, action.**

Sadly, startup websites in particular, often fall into the category of the shoemaker's shoes; the fable of the shoemaker often being the last person to get new footwear, forgetting that he himself is the product he is selling. I know your website is often low down on a list of priorities, and I know it's usually a bit of a faff to keep up to date and improve, often requiring the help of (sometimes expensive) contractors. The usual response I get from founders I work with when questioning their website is, 'It will do for now'. **Your website isn't 'for now', it's 'for the future' and so it should always point in that direction.**

33

Know The Financial Support Available

If you are an early-stage founder, it's a great idea to get yourself acquainted with the various support networks available in your country. These range from accelerators and organisations which are free of charge, to others who charge a fee or take a share of equity for a place on their programme.

These support networks will help familiarise and prepare you for the process of investment, without it feeling intimidating or alarming. This includes putting together your pitch deck, getting your materials in order and getting to grips with the many financial aids and investment incentive schemes available. In the UK the schemes often cited are SEIS and EIS. The information on these below was correct at the time of publication, however it's definitely worth checking them out in more detail as they are often updated.

With regard to SEIS and EIS, both schemes are similar, with subtle differences – the main distinction being that SEIS is for very early startups, while EIS is for more developed businesses. Both allow for angels to gain a percentage of their investment deducted from their forthcoming tax bill. This is as high as 50% with SEIS or 30% with EIS. The schemes also allow for angels to invest, with the understanding that any capital gains tax on future stock sales will be 0%. That's right, nothing. There's finally some generous loss relief included in the packages, should the investment unfortunately fail. This can be anything up to 25%, meaning that, through the scheme, if your company were to go under, an investor is in reality only risking 25% of their money. Once pre-authorisation is given from HMRC, the schemes allow for companies to gain financial backing in exchange for stock quickly, and help investors find the trust needed to take such a risk, in many cases for the very first time.

34
Reactive Momentum

W hen I speak with founders about their pitches to investors, they often discuss momentum. This could be concerns over the speed, scale of offering, or amount of interest they are receiving. They often speak about momentum as something which comes in peaks and troughs; something which sits completely outside of their control.

We've covered earlier in the book that a business sits within a society and they are afflicted by that society's problems and privileges, and yes, this can affect the momentum of a business at any stage, but only if by momentum you mean societal barriers. If, by momentum, you mean feeling, emotion, morale, direction, innovation and, in turn, power to overcome those societal barriers, then that's completely different. **Momentum is truthfully something you, as a founder, can do to the world, not just what the world does to you.**

I call this 'reactive momentum'; the realisation that we are in control of our business's direction and not just at the mercy of the world around us. Everything that has happened and will happen to your business has occurred because you started it. Everything your business has beaten or will overcome is due, at least in part, to your choices and decisions. The founders I've met who understand this principle have all had the resilience to weather tough times, and confidence in themselves and their team to make the right choices for their unique organisation.

More than anything, they have understood their capacity to affect the momentum of their business by dialling up or down the frequency of their pitching, when required. It's as straightforward as doing more, in a targeted way. This isn't easy, though. In the face of repeated rejection, or difficult conversations, doing *more* often feels like the worst thing to do. You will likely want to bury yourself in a cave and pretend you never started. Resist this urge – get up, get out, figure out why people are saying 'no', and then adapt, change, and *do more*.

There's a wonderful phrase that says, 'You can't get hit by lightning if you're not standing out in the rain'.

It's your choice to stand in the rain. It's your decision to keep pushing for momentum. It's of course paramount that you're able to do this in a way that preserves your wellbeing and doesn't lead you to burning out.

PART FOUR
OPERATIONS AND BUDGETS

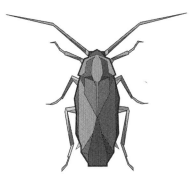

35
Cockroach Mode

In the 2008 Disney movie *WALL-E*, the world was depicted following a nuclear apocalypse, with nothing left aside from abandoned human bits and bobs, robots, and a cute little pet cockroach named Hal. You may have heard the myth that cockroaches would likely be the only living thing on Earth that would survive a world-ending event, and many studies have in fact proven that they are, to some degree, highly resilient to gamma radiation.

Why am I bringing up cockroaches? Well, not because they are gross. I was on the phone with a friend and mentor of mine the other day, Richard Thornton. Richard is an angel investor in London and an operating partner for a VC seed-stage fund. We were discussing if angels were getting 'cold feet' due to the economic downturn, and he mentioned a phrase that really struck a chord with me.

> 'For high-performing businesses to really excite and gain interest of investors, unlike perhaps anytime in recent history, they now must demonstrate their ability to enter cockroach mode *if* required. Founders today need a plan B and even C… and need to demonstrate their unit economics can work at any size and stage. The current environment for founders is tough and for the most part, it is about cash preservation for many.'

In a sense, businesses which are attracting the most interest from angels at the moment are the ones most likely to become self-reliant, or at least the ones much less reliant on future rounds of funding than perhaps was the case just a few years ago. Just like cockroaches, they have to be resilient, survivalist and very bloody difficult to kill.

This is a trend I have indeed seen reflected while working alongside founders and startups. People are finding it much harder to raise investment – however, at the same time, founders I've worked alongside have raised anything between £150,000 to £5 million, just in the last year. The money is still out there to invest.

Some of the smartest founders I know build contingency plans for 'rainy days', resist the urge to scale for the sake of scaling, and instead focus on quality over quantity. They aim to make a profit each year while in their infancy, **they make sure their model works at any scale not just at scale, and they carefully decide how much of their profit to reinvest and how much of it to save.** They 'reforecast' their budgets constantly, frequently making plans for potentially problematic events. They preserve and protect their teams at all costs, with buffer budgets they can switch on and off at will, ensuring redundancies are a last resort. They also create flexible projection models, ahead of time, which outline various different factors that can change to foresee various different outcomes.

Many of these trends have been honed and perfected during the pandemic years, when self-protection of company, people and culture were paramount, in response to the ground beneath our feet becoming more uneven than many of us had ever imagined.

36
Cash And Culture

When running a company, at any one time there are literally hundreds of things on your plate. You can often feel pulled in so many different directions, all of which feel like a priority. Focusing on what truly matters should be your only concern: cash and culture. We covered culture pretty extensively, so let's focus on cash. A thriving culture, wonderful product and engaging brand will attract customers, but take your eye off cash flow for too long and the fuel that underpins it all could perhaps begin to unravel. Focusing on what brings in the cash is crucial, especially in early-stage businesses, but developing financial materials and resources that illustrate this in a way which makes sense to you, giving you quick access to the information you need to make decisions, is even more vital.

When it comes to invoicing and contracts – don't play. **An invoice is to be treated as fuel, receipts are to be treated as cash, and contracts are to be treated as gold.** Partners (clients) may try and nudge you on this; they may pay late, or they may not sign. Short answer – don't play. If they haven't signed the contract, don't start the work. If they haven't paid their invoice, chase it. If they consistently don't pay their invoice, stop the work. If they are unhappy with anything or have delayed a project, always negotiate part payment, or better still, structure your payment terms to fixed dates rather than fixed deliverables. Always structure your payment terms with part payment upfront if you can. This will massively help as a small business, taking on the costs upfront required to proceed with the work.

There's always room for negotiation and respectful discussion, but being firm about the lifeblood of your organisation should never be seen as uncomfortable or rude. You may not be working 'just for the money', but without the money you probably wouldn't be working. A more relaxed behaviour to invoicing and payments is especially prevalent in creative industries, and certainly more likely to happen to you if you are self-employed or a freelancer. Regardless of the size of your organisation, when it comes to invoicing and payments – don't play.

This exact approach can, in fact, be applied when agreeing to any commitments that eat into your time.

It's easy to feel bombarded and overwhelmed with opportunities while scaling your organisation. We are often presented with countless options that may be great for building up our ego, but might not necessarily be ideal for building our company.

Ask yourself:

- Want to take on that speaking opportunity or podcast? **Will it contribute to your cash flow or culture?**

- Want to take that business trip abroad? **Will it contribute to your cash flow or culture?**

- Want to update your company brand and website? **Will it contribute to your cash flow or culture?**

Stay true and focused on the vitals, while of course occasionally making a little time for the 'nice to haves'.

37
Know Your Legal Responsibilities

Much of what you will be doing day-to-day as a leader will be focusing on the big picture. Very rarely throughout this book have I encouraged you to sweat the small stuff – quite the opposite, if you want to maintain a healthy work/wellbeing balance, but there are some 'small' things which should be sweated and should never be ignored. I'm talking about VAT, corporation tax, insurance, payment deadlines, payroll and your government numbers and logins. As the founder, your legal directorial responsibilities may not be the most exciting part of the job, they may not even be your natural skillset (who really enjoys filling out a tax return?) but they are certainly some of the most important.

Miss a tax payment deadline and you may lose sight of what your accurate cash flow position looks like. File an incorrect VAT return and you could risk a hefty fine, a lengthy and tiresome investigation, or at worst, criminal proceedings with up to seven years in prison (in the UK).

These legal responsibilities are in place to make sure your company is fulfilling its obligations and giving back to the community and society it serves. There are tons of professionals who can help you with these tasks, including sending you reminders for deadlines or processing duties on your behalf. They, hopefully, are also clued up on the most recent incentives such as tax credits/breaks, claimable expenses, and accounting techniques, that should help your business make the most of these schemes.

38
Chasing Your Tail

There's a phenomenon in business which occurs most often when organisations over-sell and under-service, when they commit to more than they have the capacity or resources to deliver on and they begin 'chasing their tail'. They perhaps need to bring in new business to pay for commitments they have already made, but those commitments require more commitments, which then require more new business. It's an endless cycle.

We're often taught by online entrepreneurs to 'say yes and then work out the details later'. An element of this mindset helps us to secure new contracts, and scales our company effectively. Don't know how to do something? Say yes, and figure it out along the way. This is part of the entrepreneurial mindset; a by-product of the 'always adapting, always learning' approach, and it avoids huge dips in your workflow and circumvents paying for team members without work for them to complete – but only to an extent. If 50-75% of your business is operating in this tail-chasing fashion, you don't have a sustainable company.

It's the age-old question – do we hire before the curve or after the curve? Do we build capacity for what is to come, or wait for it to happen and then build it? The answer comes down to the accuracy and malleability of your financial projections, the adaptability of your team, your buffer for unforeseen circumstances and your ability to reverse decisions as a last resort. If you have sufficient cash flow and can accurately forecast an effective runway, then hiring ahead of the curve, ahead of the new business, is always my preference, but this can be a quick way to go out of business – so be careful. Again, ensuring you're billing as much cash flow upfront will help you to make these kinds of decisions in good faith.

Overselling, under-serving and chasing your tail isn't just an issue that crops up with the work your company does, it also creeps into the importance of how your work is communicated. This is even more important if your work fails. I'm sure we've all heard the warning that we should never over-promise and under-deliver. The way your organisation communicates to the community it serves, and the way it finds that voice, is vital to the trust your customers and partners will have in you.

To give an example, early on in 2023, Virgin Orbit launched the first-ever space mission from UK soil. The rocket carrying the payload (in this case, a series of satellites) was launched from Cornwall, onboard a retro-fitted Boeing 747, named 'Cosmic Girl'. The plan was for the plane to climb to a staggering altitude and then release the rocket into orbit. It would have been a monumental moment for the UK and Western Europe, joining the space race. Unfortunately, the launch didn't just end in failure, it was communicated incredibly poorly.

To a large extent, companies such as SpaceX have set the bar incredibly high, not just for successful space missions, but for how these missions are documented, story-told and communicated, across multiple platforms and channels. We've watched drone footage of rockets taking off and landing, perfectly lit with thunderous soundtracks to boot. We've also seen countless shots of their mission control centres, with high ceilings and rows of glossy workstations. The expectation was therefore very high for this first mission from UK soil, and to their credit, Virgin Orbit released beautiful press shots ahead of the launch, showing 'Cosmic Girl' drop launching the rocket in daylight, perfectly lit and full of the drama and wonder you'd expect.

Which is why, it wasn't so much disappointing that the first Virgin Orbit mission failed to reach orbit – that's part and parcel of the investment in space technology – but more disappointing in how the world watched it fail. In short, no one was able to see anything. We were treated to a disjointed live stream, with confused presenters, misinformation, all with dark and unclear camera footage that actually missed the event of the drop launch. We saw 'Cosmic Girl' rip along a runway to take off in complete darkness, with only one wobbly, long-distance camera shot. To top it off, we kept being treated to what looked like security camera footage from the corner of mission control, which looked like a school classroom with messy computer desks, dodgy tea and coffee flasks and a pop-up banner display seemingly depicting the conditions of code red or green. A far cry from the expectations the majority of their audience harboured.

In many ways it was a masterclass reminder that it doesn't matter so much whether you fail, that's how you learn; what matters more is how you communicate while failing in order to avoid chasing your tail. **Knowledge of what your customers and community expect, and managing those expectations with clear communication, is crucial to avoiding over-promising and under-delivering.**

39
Invest In Your People

Just as an angel may invest in you as a research and development project – an asset which they hope will increase in value over time – so must you invest in your team. Staff members are not just paid in line with what their role is worth, they are paid with respect to how much it would cost to replace them, and how much value they individually bring to your company culture and impact. It's your job to increase that value, and then pay them accordingly to reflect this.

In real-world terms, this means building in budget lines that accommodate training and development opportunities, while also creating processes for team members to bring such opportunities to senior management to seek funding. **It also means tying individual financial success to company success.**

This includes having commission and bonus schemes that are linked to overall profit, if targets are met, and perhaps even going further, making a budget available for team members to start their own private projects, which fuel and tie into the overall mission of the organisation.

At my own company, I started a scheme called the 'History Shaper Program'. This made a fixed percentage of total annual turnover available to all team members to create their own social impact projects. The company would hold competition days for our people to pitch their ideas, with the winning pitch being commissioned and the full weight of the agency being promised to support it. This led to the company supporting initiatives to end marriage discrimination in Northern Ireland, lower the cost of emergency contraception in the UK, fundraise hundreds of thousands of pounds at Christmas for a children's hospice and encourage the *Daily Mail* to begin to use inclusive, progressive language when reporting on trans youth. These campaigns were **the outward expression of the essence of the company**, and the financial commitment behind them meant our team members were able to grow, develop and try new things.

40
Budget Transparency

If you would like to create a culture and a team that each fuel the success of your business, they first need to understand your business. If you want to nurture and enrich a group of people and help them engage in the entrepreneurial spirit that powers your organisation, you have to be brave enough to show them your organisation and help them understand its inner workings.

I often see budget-transparency schemes introduced at companies with the aim of providing clarity, only to add more confusion. Some organisations may share with their employees their top-line revenue targets, they may even make public their pre- or post-tax profit (rarely), but the parts in between are often completely redacted. How does someone in your organisation know where they stand if they don't know how their own value corresponds to the total value of the company? How can they engage in the entrepreneurial spirit if the details of entrepreneurial decisions are being withheld from them?

At my company, we make public to our team not just our top-line or bottom-line numbers, but all the numbers in between. For example, our people know the cost of our office lease, at a time when the value of physical space has never been more prevalent. They also know everyone else's salaries. This knowledge empowers them with a greater and broader outlook on what they are building.

Our salary-transparency policy makes public the salary bracket for any job description. It also ensures all staff know every remuneration category within the company. These are reviewed on an annual basis and tweaked to ensure they stay in line with industry standards.

We also discuss salaries within a structure that encourages autonomy. All roles within the company are split into specialisms, not hierarchies, and the leadership is constructed of mentors, not managers. This allows for everyone in the organisation to be accountable, while also harbouring and encouraging a culture of support, help, and genuine teamwork. While all mentors should always have their mentees' backs, *no matter what*, this structure also helps avoid any toxic 'blame games' that too often get passed up and down the food chain in traditional businesses. Every team member becomes accountable and, hopefully, empowered.

Every year, everyone within the organisation is encouraged to write a salary proposal to be shared and discussed with their mentor against industry benchmarks. Over the years, this process has been refined with the help of employee feedback, so that our people are given clear guidance and support throughout this process. Mentees fill out separate proposals alongside their mentors, and then meet to compare and contrast. It's important that this process is completed in tandem first, and then in collaboration.

Similarly, our people don't just have fixed salaries, **their success is embedded into the success of the organisation**, with commissions and bonuses that help them succeed as the business does. We also engage our people with share option agreements, inviting key individuals to join an EMI scheme (Enterprise Management Incentive), allowing them to benefit in the future success of the company, as its other shareholders do.

The overall lesson we have learnt is that **salary transparency doesn't just improve team performance or loyalty, it fuels the overall success of the business**. When you empower your team to speak confidently about their own value, you train them to think and speak with commerciality, and for some people that will be for the very first time. This mindset carries through to their approach to work, and, hopefully, also to your bottom line.

Salary transparency doesn't just help to nurture a cash-savvy team, it also goes at least some way to tackling our generation's most challenging issues concerning equity in the workplace. We can no longer ignore that we live in a world where women often under-sell themselves when applying for jobs, and both women and people from marginalised groups and communities often get offered far less lucrative opportunities or fair remuneration. In this regard, schemes that help people speak openly about money at work endeavour to level the playing field in terms of gender and race, although we've got a long way to go.

Many organisations shy away from this process for fear of opening a can of worms, but the idea is catching on. New York and Colorado have recently passed laws requiring all employers to disclose salary ranges on every job description. Agreed, salary transparency can be extremely delicate to implement and many people are used to cultures which keep salaries a secret. In my very first job in retail, I wasn't allowed to speak about my salary with anyone. My silence was written into my contract and I could have been fired for speaking up. With a little patience, persistence and goodwill, however, building a more transparent and open approach to your business's finances will empower your team to think and behave more commercially, while also fuelling the business's success as a whole. This in turn further creates an autonomous organisation; one that is solving problems and making decisions independent of its founder – helping you concentrate on your core responsibilities and avoiding you and others from burning out.

41
Be Time Mindful

Just as we need to become mindful of our actions, we should also consider becoming more mindful of our time. Aside from selling a product or service, as a leader you are mostly selling your time. Plenty of organisations, including startups, track, measure and optimise their employees' time to ensure efficiency, but how many founders and leaders do the same for their own? Perhaps very few.

Those I've worked with who treat themselves as their own employee, complete with time measurement, are the ones that, by and large, are most successful. This doesn't have to be meticulous, it can be based on estimations – but some degree of **knowledge of time spent is crucial, to then decide if it's been time well spent.**

Founders and leaders must learn to manage and mentor themselves, in the same way they compassionately and consciously manage and shepherd others. I've known companies who don't price out their founder's time, even though the individual is, in effect, doing three people's jobs at once until they get more funding. Learning and observing the value of your time as a leader will enable you to make better choices, deciding which tasks you eventually assign to others, when you do this, and how much that time is worth. To grow a sustainable business, one that also reaches a stable and reliable valuation, all tasks and roles required to power that organisation need to be budgeted and paid for, regardless of who is doing them.

I've spoken at length about automation throughout this book. It's one of my guiding principles. When it comes to time, however, there is something a founder should never automate, and that's their diary. I know it's trendy to use software that allows others to book out our time, but even if that time has been stipulated as bookable, what we're really doing by opening up our diary to a piece of software is giving others power and authority over our priorities. It may feel like the time you spend manually booking meetings is a laborious use of energy that could be better spent elsewhere, but it's well worth those moments of consideration. **Founders who see their diary as their to-do list, with each task they need to complete assigned a duration, are more conscious of their performance, aware of their responsibilities and remain**

more focused on their vision. Allow your time to be divvied-up on a first-come, first-served basis, and risk diluting the integrity of your company.

Your inbox, on the other hand, that's fair game for automation. Using services like Slack (https://slack.com/intl/en-gb) or Trello (https://trello.com), which dedicate communication to a particular task, allow us to avoid using email for project management or team discussion. For me, email is primarily a tool for external communication; namely, for new business and partnerships. To do this well, over the years I have become almost entirely reliant on one thing – the block button. I block ruthlessly. Who wants to rely on an untrustworthy unsubscribe, when you're certain you never subscribed in the first place? An email inbox has a clear function and when we allow others to invade that space, we risk that function being eroded. When your email inbox is your strongest mechanism for developing new business relationships and securing meetings, not ruthlessly automating it can mean less of what you want and more of what you don't.

I refer to these tactics as 'consciousness management'. Where do we want to place our consciousness and how can we keep it there, minimising the risk of interruption?

I'm sure we've all heard the phrase 'that meeting could have been an email', but perhaps a better mantra for a founder is 'that meeting should have been more predictable'. The companies I've worked within, and now advise, all create detailed meeting agendas well in advance, to ensure everyone knows what they are walking into. No one is going to perform at their best when they are faced with a surprise, and often, regardless of people's competencies, you'll get much more value from your team if you give them advance notice of what is to be discussed. This is especially true for founders, who, as I've said, often take on many roles at once as the company is scaling. My pet hate is getting emails asking for 'ten minutes of my time to discuss something super important'. Talk about a cliffhanger! As a founder, knowing what you are walking into with enough notice to prepare for it can help you be the best version of yourself in that meeting, for your own wellbeing but also for the wellbeing of those around you.

42
Purpose And Profit

I 'll say this just once: **it's entirely possible and likely that you will profit from running your business purposefully.** This is for your team, being mindful of their own ambitions and circumstances, for your customers and partners, but also for the planet and the wider community your business serves. As we've already discussed, the businesses currently securing the most investment are those that are seeking to purposefully solve real-world problems and generate real-world positive social impact.

When I set up my business, I did so under the structure of a limited company. I found the limitations of other more purpose-specific structures, such as a community interest company or a non-profit, too stifling. The business, at its core, was about communicating, amplifying and accelerating the social impact of activists, organisations and institutions. It therefore didn't need a specific structure dedicated to ensuring that happened. Sure, it would have made us able to take donations for our work, but that was never the business model.

I knew the business was going to be profit making, because I was building a vehicle that would not only seek to change my life, but change the lives of our people, all the while providing a best-practice example of how this can be done for others. I wanted to create an organisation that would build social impact leaders, not just helping our partners, but actually helping our own people achieve this and grow. This is why I hired people who had potential but weren't at their peak. I wanted them to mature as the business did. I saw my organisation, from the very beginning, as an opportunity to build something that builds others, on a self-perpetuating model that fuels growth, and aims to go some way to providing financial, physical and emotional security for everyone involved.

To do all of this, my business had to make a profit. While building your business, you will be faced with countless obstacles that risk the viability of your margins, but stick to your guns. A business dedicated to healthy profit (and a healthy moral compass to boot) develops, in time, the freedom to carve out its own path and empowers others to do the same. This mindset allowed us to invest in team growth ahead of the curve, often before we had secured new revenue. It allowed us to take educated risks and create a culture where our team could fail as they innovated. Lastly, it enabled me to empower and work with my senior team to gradually take autonomy of the entire organisation, and eventually allow me to exit the business. This is where our next section kicks off...

PART FIVE
SELLING YOUR BUSINESS

43
Don't Build
A Beautiful Cage

Y ou'll be tempted, as you start and scale your business, to look around you from time to time and
admire what you've created. To you, and hopefully to
the many others it serves and supports, it should be
beautiful. This isn't just an exercise to serve your ego
(hopefully, far from it), but instead one to serve your
soul. It's important to take stock of our story's achievements.

In these moments of observation, no matter how
closely we look, we likely won't see the bars of the
cage around this beautiful thing we've created – we're
taught to ignore them. Worse still, when we admire
another person's business, we witness its ambition
and achievements, but rarely get to see the extent to
which it has truly trapped its founder.

For this reason, when we build our own business, we must remain mindful of the potential for exit and be wary of the beautiful cage. It's not a case of always needing to have a getaway car ready with its engine idling; at times you should be able to go for months, if not years, without giving it too much thought at all. To some degree, however, you should have a plan to automate out of your own business when you seek to do so.

For many years while scaling my company, eventually selling it wasn't something on my radar. I wanted to grow a lifestyle business that meant something to many people, including myself. Why would I ever leave that? For this reason, I've often found myself giving the advice that **we should never scale our businesses with the sole destination of selling them**, this will damage their core integrity. We should build our businesses on the idea that we would want to work for them forever, and then we don't. That's how you build businesses that other people want to work for.

As founders, for many reasons, many of us end up falling in love with our companies. We adore them, which is why we work on them tirelessly, but there is a fine line between love and possession. While your business might be something you own, it must never become something which owns you. Many of the founders I've met over the years have worked hard to detangle themselves from something that once was indistinguishable from their identity. Their business has somehow found its way into every area of their lives. This process of detachment can take a long time, which is why it's important to create your vision for selling as early on as possible, and then come to terms with the patience required to see it through.

It's not just your team that will have to detach themselves from you, ensuring processes and decisions can be taken without your involvement – the trickiest part of any exit is detaching yourself emotionally from your creation. Who are you without your business? When you go to events or dinner parties and you sit next to someone new, how are you 'interesting' if you don't have your business to speak about? This is the true beautiful cage – and **the trick is choosing to detach, while knowing the comfort of staying**. The key is knowing you are enough, without your business.

44

Exits Aren't One Size Fits All

While we build companies for others – vehicles for other people's success – it's crucial to keep in mind what we would like our businesses to achieve for ourselves. We're rarely encouraged to be selfish when developing as leaders; it seldom helps any situation – but when selling your business, while the process is collaborative, it should also be deeply personal and, at times, a deeply selfish experience. As I write those words, I dislike them, but it's true. With the best will in the world, even when working with the most respectful of buyers, **you are the only one at the negotiating table looking out for your own interests**. Exits are probably the only moment in our progression as leaders when we must look inward to what we need so we end up receiving enough to be able to step away. Once you've signed and got paid, there's no going back, so that number has to feel right for you.

For this reason, selling your business and going through an exit is an inherently intimate experience. It has the power to unlock financial resources and free time which can change your life, and perhaps help you to go on to start other businesses, with boundless potential. Exits are not one size fits all, and while it's vital to speak to and get counsel from others who have gone through the experience themselves, it's also important that you're able to feel like **you can choose the best path for you, which might not be the path most trodden.**

We explored in the Prologue the usual routes that people select. An MBO is a Management Buy Out where the existing management of the company are able to buy your shares in the business. An EOT is an Employee Ownership Trust, which is set up to purchase your shareholdings. These are then held in a trust on behalf of all the staff at the company. (If you're from the UK, think of the John Lewis model.) EOTs are increasingly popular routes for founders, as they provide impressive tax incentives for capital gains received. Lastly, there is the Trade Sale. This is usually the most common choice for exiting founders as it involves another business or group of companies buying your shareholdings. It usually fetches the most in terms of value, however it often comes along with tricky earn-outs, that tie founders into periods of working for the company with impossibly high targets and little control. If these aren't met, their full payout isn't received. Trade sales also risk the integrity of your business being watered down, or even the business being dissolved entirely.

Whichever route you choose, it is your own choice to make and the process of making this decision should take you considerable time. It's often helpful to employ the support of a mediator, someone who's seasoned in company sales and knows the intricacies. They can stand beside you throughout the process and advise, potentially all parties if they are willing, helping navigate the inevitably difficult conversations that will arise.

45
Valuation Myths

Just as we shouldn't find ourselves comparing our success too closely with our competitors, when we begin to sell our business, one of the worst things we can do is compare our valuation to others. **Valuations are subjective, topical and, above all, not just a reflection of your business, but also a reflection of the market your company serves and supports.** If you have worked hard to make your business unique, to ensure it's genuinely fit for purpose, then discerning its valuation through comparison is almost impossible.

There are many ways you can find a company valuation; some bear in mind a multiple of revenue and others multiply profit. This is just a starting point before the valuation goes much deeper into the inner workings of your organisation. There are qualified professionals who will assist you and help you find various benchmarks. Some routes may be more lucrative than others but hold greater risk.

Throughout this process of valuation you will probably come to understand that, as a founder, you have overvalued your own organisation in your mind. We've all done it. We open Google and type, 'what multiple of EBITDA should I sell my business for?', and then begin to see crazy and unrealistic formulas that would probably be laughed out of the negotiation room. Try as hard as you can to remain realistic. Businesses that fetch huge multiples are likely to be the very top 1% of most deals. They are often unicorns that make up a tiny percentage of the life-changing, successful deals that happen each and every day. Engaging in the curse of comparison is, quite frankly, bonkers. The key to honing a good price for your company is balance.

I'll be honest with you, **great deals that happen are far better than absolutely amazing deals that don't.** One pays out, the other doesn't – no matter how hard the founder has worked. Let's make sure you strike a deal that actually closes, and doesn't just look good on paper. In short, there's no point getting a valuation that nobody will entertain, because your business is really only worth what someone else is willing to pay for it.

The process of finding your accurate valuation, at any stage of scale but especially at exit, is one of accepting home truths. As I've already said in this book, the sooner you can reach clarity, the better chance you have of making choices that bring you the level of success you are looking for and that's right for you.

46
Sell Slowly – Start Early

One of the best ways to raise your valuation is to create a business that is autonomous of its founder. If I purchase your company and then have to work with you for five years in order to get the true value of the knowledge acquired, the business is worth far less than if we can shake hands and wave goodbye on day one. Of course, as mentioned, many deals include an 'earnout' as part of the negotiation, which means the founder and/or selling partner must stay working at the business for a period of time to ensure targets are met and a swift and smooth transition. Earn-outs are a great option for helping deals to complete successfully, but if your business is able to operate independently of yourself right away, the company is immediately worth more.

With this in mind, many founders race towards the exit, tripping up over themselves along the way. A better approach is to sell slowly, and start as early as possible. Your route to exit should start the day you make your first hire, because that's the first time you are testing automation, and empowering decision making in someone else. The route to scaling a business isn't as simple as rinse and repeat thereafter, but if you're able to carefully, compassionately and consciously make choices that shift power and authority away from yourself, and then test if it works, then this is the best way to craft a company and culture that is self-sustaining. This process of handing over takes time, often many years, so begin detaching yourself from the business early, little by little, retaking control when detachments don't work out, constantly getting feedback to help improvements when they do.

We've already explored the concept of making yourself dispensable. This is where this lesson can take full effect, should you be able to put it into action. Fight the artificial urgency to race towards the successful exit, and instead craft something that truly works for the community it serves, and also for you.

47
Know Your Red Lines

The experience of selling your company can be highly emotional. Discussions may build you up as they tear you down. You'll watch as your lifeblood is praised yet scrutinised, commended yet critiqued, touted yet trivialised. These are all natural stages of any exit negotiation. For the deal to be successful, all parties should be open to these discussions, and compassionate to compromise. But they also should know their red lines, and stick to them.

There may be countless respectful disagreements and discussions throughout the course of your exit. This is a good thing – because it means all parties genuinely care about the deal's viability. It means that the seller understands the true value of their business, and the buyer wants to make sure what they are purchasing will be successful. It's good to expect these challenges and **approach them with a sense of perspective and compassion.**

Your job is to **pick your battles and know what you want to get from the deal, for you personally.** This includes for your family, friends and loved ones; whoever will also be impacted by your exit being successful. Often, when seeking our red lines, it's useful to picture the people behind the contracts and clauses, those we care about most – this humanises the impact of our choices. For your exit to be a success, and for it to benefit the people you love, you must only have a handful of red lines. Stay true to what you won't budge on, and compromise on everything else.

As the legal documents are drawn up, discussed and amended, be sure that your red lines remain constant. This is where your mediator can help hugely, ensuring everyone's ideals are met. The various contracts you'll sign (and there will be many), will provide a framework for future communication and compromises. They should lay out a route and structure that determines the future processes of the business, including how disagreements are resolved.

It's always best practice to approach these documents with the mindset that, while relationships are strong now, at some point in the future, with the best will in the world, they may break down, and when that happens all parties need a fail-safe. While day-to-day these contracts provide a great resource and reminder of decisions agreed upon, if you ever truly need the documents, much of what was once secured in order to seal the deal will have already been lost. Therefore, post-sale, it's your responsibility to ensure that relationships remain strong, all participants are accountable, and all decisions are subject to compromise. This is part of being a compassionate and conscious leader, as much as an emotionally intelligent negotiator.

48

Running The Business As You Sell

You may have automated most of your daily tasks, and the business is hopefully running independent of yourself as much as possible. It's a self-perpetuating organism that scales on its own, but even when you get to this stage, there will still be countless tasks that only you can do as the business owner. Much of this will be directorial responsibilities and your governmental duties, and frankly, there's no getting out of that.

While you're balancing the needs and wants of all the parties involved in a deal, you will most likely be also balancing the various needs and demands of the business. If you ignore the company for too long, you risk it failing and then impacting the deal. If you focus on the company and not the deal, you'll never get your exit past the finish line.

With this in mind, it's crucial that you're honest and open with your senior management team about the prospect of a sale, and, if you're able to, your wider team as well. If they have share options in the business, it will be in their best interests to help it perform at its best, because their agreements will likely only kick in at the point of an exit or merger. It's in everyone's interest therefore to support each other, and for them to support you as you navigate an uncertain road through this tricky venture.

It's also worth noting that the business may be negatively affected if your deal takes too long to complete. While you shouldn't rush the process, if anyone is holding things up unnecessarily, it's definitely within your interest, and within your authority, to nudge things along.

49
Post-Sale Fatigue And Fire

You've exited your business and you've come out the other side. What do you do now? Firstly, you will most likely want to mark the moment in some sort of ceremonial way. Many founders go on once-in-a-lifetime trips, enjoying the time away from their responsibilities (and their screens) for the first time in what may feel like forever. Others like to be among family and friends, invest in other people's businesses, and/or give a proportion of their capital gains away to charity. In whatever way you find yourself marking the moment, it's important to do so. You've worked exceptionally hard to reach this point in your career, and your life, and the impact of your consistent and conscious grind should be both rewarded and remembered.

Few people reach this level of success, and even fewer do so with their wellbeing intact. Relationships with others and even ourselves are often burnt along the way, so reaching this moment and being able to share it with those you love and care about is crucial.

I guarantee you, the next thing you'll do will be some sort of extreme activity or sport, or something that pushes your mind, body and soul to their limits. So many successful people do this when they reach a form of 'finish line', because our minds aren't the type that are naturally or easily encouraged to slow down. **We've worked at the top of our game for years, and now we want that same buzz from something else** – perhaps something we've been longing to do or achieve our entire lives, and now we have the time, space and money to indulge. I'm not here to tell you *not* to do this – I found myself climbing mountains and pushing myself in extreme off-road cycling.

The advice I would give is to try and remain conscious of yourself and mindful of the lessons in this book. If we witness our decisions and are aware of why they are being made, a healthy approach is definitely to monitor our behaviour, but also to enjoy. There's no harm in trying to achieve something new, as long as you don't beat yourself up when you fail at it – which you will, because failure is the only way people really learn something new.

Do things which make your heart truly sing, and invest your time and energy into passions which don't automatically bring you validation, praise, attention or income. This might be the first time in your life you don't have to worry about financial security. Instead of running to set up another business, enjoy the moment first, and indulge in activities you've always wanted to spend more time doing. I spent a lot of time travelling to new countries, exploring new cultures and learning new lessons. I bought a piano the day after my company sold; something I've loved since my childhood. I now sit most evenings and tinkle on the keys, perhaps writing a piece of music that will only be heard by my own ears. In the same way, try to engage in things which you truly love but which won't bring you the type of success you've perhaps become accustomed to. These moments of undriven satisfaction can be some of the most rewarding.

A lot about that post-sale phase is about balancing fatigue with fire. You will find yourself a hell of a lot less busy than you once were, than you have perhaps ever been. You may also find yourself exhausted from the experience of selling. This can all be disconcerting and, in some cases, anxiety inducing. Who are we if we aren't building our business and working towards our success? The truth is that this is a moment – an opportunity – to truly find out. **That's the true gift of an exit: not financial freedom, but emotional freedom.**

The truth is, if you are destined to start another business, you will do so, in time. There's no hurry. That fire that existed in you, which encouraged you to begin building a company all those years ago, will continue to exist in you – only now you have the opportunity to build something with the perspective of emotional freedom.

Of course, you will feel the tendency to look back towards the company you have sold. Perhaps this is because you remain a shareholder, because you are working through an earnout, or just because you care about its success. Don't be offended as you watch your creation slowly – or in some cases pretty rapidly – transform. The organisation will begin to look like the reflection of its new owners, and we hope it's all the better and stronger for it. Nevertheless, it can be an unsettling experience, because we will undoubtedly be watching as the decisions, choices and successes of yesterday take on less and less value. Remember, this doesn't mean you are not valued. You are, and what you have created is of great value to those who now work for and steer the ship.

You now have a choice: what do you do next?

To reach true success, it is often said that we must be able to get up each morning and do the same thing, repeatedly. This is true, but truly sustainable success is being able to get up each morning and choose where we place our energy. This is now your mission.

EPILOGUE

50
Know Your Limits, And Push Them

Your power as a founder lies in your empowerment of others, and yourself. Your influence as a leader blooms as you understand your people and then help them achieve mastery. Your legacy as an entrepreneur is calcified as you accept your own imperfections and use that knowledge to scale something healthy.

Your company is the vehicle you use to achieve these great things, and your wellbeing is the foundation that makes it all possible. The biggest part of this endeavour is learning what greatness truthfully means for each of us. Push too far, and live someone else's version of success, push too little and live with the feelings of lost potential.

To build a company that bosses it without burnout, and to grow an organisation without damaging your wellbeing, you must look to **strengthen your belief that you are enough**. You alone, without any of the success or the validation that comes with it, or the inevitable ties to emotional, physical and financial security; just you, alone, are enough.

Once you build from there, you see that your power and your potential lie not in how you scale success, but in how you share it. It's how you balance your comfort zone with your peace. It's how you push your limits, while knowing your limits. It's knowing you are always climbing, even when it feels like you're falling. It's believing that growing something for other people will in turn cultivate something for yourself.

As you choose to start, scale or sell a company, know that these choices carry both risk and reward. It's a risk to everything you hold dear and everything you're yet to discover, but if chosen consciously and openly, without ego and without pretension, it's **a reward to live free from the many troubles that have inspired you to start this journey in the first place**.

I've often thought that, if we could see ourselves from above, from an altitude high enough to witness not just the impact of our own actions, but the impact of everyone we've ever met, it would be obvious why we make the choices we make, and aspire to reach the levels of success we think will bring us happiness.

From this elevation, with time sped up, we could perhaps see an entire lifetime's map of interactions; every connection influencing others; every action rippling outward.

While we can't look upon our own lives with this sense of height and scale, perhaps we don't need to in order to grasp a degree of the same perspective. Your life, your success, your choices, are all the result of thousands of interactions, many of which you will never see, touch or understand. Perhaps the greatest lesson of them all is trusting the humble influence of inevitability, and the scale of our potential to influence others for the better. All we then need to do is step out into the world and be truthfully and honestly ourselves. When we do this, we aren't just building our own stories, we're helping build everyone else's as well.

Keep climbing – keep building. Keep on keeping on, with an open mind, an open heart, and hold on to the idea that your business can change the lives of many, including your own, for the better.

Acknowledgements

This book is the product of a personal transformational journey, one I'm so grateful for and one I wouldn't have been able to achieve without the support and help from trusted friends, family and co-workers. For this, first and foremost, I must thank, as always, my confidant and my mother, Jan, whose endless support and love have always meant the most to me. I extend my thanks also to my grandmother, Diane, whose countless discussions distilled the many lessons in this book. I consider my life blessed to be, so often, led by two such strong matriarchs. Lastly, I thank my father, Angelo. This book, inadvertently, not only helped transform my life but also helped transform our relationship – something I'll always be grateful for. What more can a son hope for than to better understand the depth of the footsteps he follows?

Antony, Dominic, Olivia – keep climbing. Keep building. Love you.

I deeply appreciate and thank the guidance and love of my three (adopted) sisters, Sophie, Nathalie and Jennifer. You've kept me on task as I've penned this. Thank you for always pointing me due north.

And to Kyle – it turns out all I had to do was walk (and write!). As I say so often to you, I feel only gratitude.

I would particularly like to thank Lauren and Ed, my co-captains at Shape History, and trusted friends and advisors. Scaling an international social impact agency with you both has been one of life's most rewarding and affirming experiences, one I'm excited to be supporting now from the wings. I'll be forever grateful for your support and guidance.

My thanks go out to *Founder Therapy*'s many interviewees, partners, test readers, experts, illustrators and content creators. You gave your time, voice, skill and energy to something that will hopefully help so many others. It's so much more than just a book.

A special thanks to Jerry. That short conversation in 2020 really did change my life.

And to you… the reader. Make of this what you will, but also will yourself to make something great.

References

1   Close Brothers, 'Facts & Figures – UK SMEs'
    (1 July 2021) www.closeassetfinance.co.uk/
    CBBF-insights/facts-figures-uk-smes, accessed
    17 March 2023
2   Freeman, M, *Are Entrepreneurs 'Touched with
    Fire'?* (UCSF, 2015)
3   *The Deloitte Global Millennial Survey 2019,*
    Deloitte (2019) www2.deloitte.com/content/
    dam/Deloitte/global/Documents/About-
    Deloitte/deloitte-2019-millennial-survey.pdf,
    accessed 17 March 2023
4   Van Hagan, I, 'Show this graph to anyone who
    thinks "young people have never had it this
    easy"', *Indy100* (24 October 2020) www.indy100.
    com/news/affordable-housing-prices-uk-graph-

cost-young-people-renting-9723124, accessed 17 March 2023

5 Kiyosaki, K, 'In the school system, they don't want us to learn about money' (18 November 2021), https://fb.watch/kE77T97APm

6 Bethune, S, 'Stress in America: Pandemic impedes basic decision-making ability', *American Psychological Association* (25 October 2021) www.apa.org/news/press/releases/2021/10/stress-pandemic-decision-making, accessed 14 March 2023

7 Hari, J, *Lost Connections: Why you're depressed and how to find hope* (Bloomsbury Circus, 2018)

8 Colonna, J, *Reboot: Leadership and the art of growing up* (HarperBus, 2019)

9 Manson, M, *The Subtle Art of Not Giving a F*ck: A counterintuitive approach to living a good life* (HarperCollins, 2016)

10 '1. Experiences build brain architecture', Center on the Developing Child at Harvard University (2011) www.youtube.com/watch?v=VNNsN9IJkws&t=113s, accessed 14 March 2023

11 Freeman, M, *Are Entrepreneurs 'Touched with Fire'?* (UCSF, 2015)

12 Emmons, RA, *Thanks! How the new science of gratitude can make you happier* (HarperOne, 2007)

13 Wax, R, *A Mindfulness Guide To Survival* (Welbeck, 2021); Wax, R, 'The Ruby Wax Mindfulness Course' (2021) www.facebook.

com/watch/?v=1419185091808626, accessed
14 March 2023

14 Wax, R, *A Mindfulness Guide To Survival*
(Welbeck, 2021)

15 Heimans, J and Timms, H, *New Power: How
power works in our hyperconnected world – and how
to make it work for you* (Picador, 2018)

16 Emmons, RA, *Thanks! How the new science of
gratitude can make you happier* (HarperOne, 2007)

17 Radvansky, GA and Copeland, DE, 'Walking
through doorways causes forgetting: Situations
models and experienced space', Memory &
Cognition, 34/5 (2006) 1150-6 DOI: 10.3758/
bf03193261

18 Buehner, CW, *Richard Evans' Quote Book*
(Publisher's Press, 1971)

19 Hari, J, *Lost Connections* (Bloomsbury Circus, 2018)

The Author

Mike Buonaiuto is a philanthropic business leader and performance coach who founded, scaled and exited Shape History, the award-winning social impact agency, working alongside global institutions including the United Nations, Atlantic Council and World Health Organization.

He's currently a senior advisor helping companies nurture their people, navigate growth and negotiate pivotal moments of transformation. Mike also supports Virgin Startup as their 'Entrepreneur In Residence' and NatWest's Business Accelerator.

His TEDx talk, 'No wonder people are quitting – business must do better' was selected and featured by TED's Editor picks. Mike lives in London and spends his time between home and New York City.

🌐 www.MikeBuonaiuto.com

in www.linkedin.com/in/mike-buonaiuto

◎ http://instagram.com/mike_shapes